Dear Hearts

Dear Hearts

Conversations with Presbyterians

Interviews by Vic Jameson

Presbyterian Publishing House
Louisville, Kentucky

This book is for Don Brown,
who made it possible,
and for Frances, who made it fun

Book design by Drew Stevens

Cover design by Peyton Talbott III

First edition

Published by Presbyterian Publishing House
Louisville, Kentucky

To order call 800/227–2872
Item # 00941084

PRINTED IN THE UNITED STATES OF AMERICA

9 8 7 6 5 4 3 2 1

Contents ❦

Foreword 🖤

Naming this book was the hardest part of writing it.

Interviewing the Presbyterians whose stories make up the book was a delight.Writing the stories was easy: Just about all that was necessary was to put down what people said.

Deciphering hastily written notes wasn't always easy. On the day I was hired to be editor of *Presbyterian Survey* magazine a brand-new colleague, preparing to leave a meeting room, paused and looked over my shoulder at my scribbles. With a shake of her head and amazing candor, she said, "Sure hope you can type."

That was years ago; my note-taking hasn't gotten any better.

But naming the book was something else again.

In its embryonic existence it was spoken of as "Ordinary Presbyterians." But Presbyterians aren't ordinary.

Call it "Real Presbyterians," maybe? Not bad, but it implies that some aren't real.

"Listening to Presbyterians" came to mind—and the book sure enough is a result of a lot of listening. But book titles need to sing—to attract attention, to invite the passerby in bookstore or library to pause for a longer look. "Listening . . . " doesn't seem to do that.

So, it is called what it is called in an effort to describe honestly what is in it, what it tries to be: A few good stories told by Presbyterians whose names, in most cases, aren't nationwide household words; people who make up the heart and the backbone of the church.

Books like this can't possibly be up-to-date. People graduate from school, change jobs, get married, move from one place to another. All in the time between concept and conclusion of a book's publication.

Some of those things have happened to some of the people in this book. You may find them in places or positions different from those described. Despite continued efforts at accuracy, some of the data are sure to have a touch of unreality.

But the stories, like the people, are real.

Steve Young 🍒

He was graduated from Mississippi State University with a degree in chemical engineering, and soon afterward he had a job with a computer consulting firm. But neither of those vocations really satisfied him. So in 1991 he left his job to take his risks at doing what he had wanted to do all along: "to devote my time to songwriting."

Stephen Edward Young,—"I go by Steve"—acquired much of his love for music from or through his maternal grandfather. "He was very musical. He played guitar and taught me to play guitar when I was 10. It's hard not to have that sort of thing rub off."

His grandfather had a great influence on him in other ways while Steve was growing up in Tupelo, Mississippi, including his being a Presbyterian. "He taught a series on the lectionary in the men's class, and had been on the session for about twelve terms (about thirty-six years). Church was his life."

Steve's parents are equally active. His father has been "a Sunday school teacher as long as I can remember," and his mother sings in the choir. Steve observes that "I probably do too much" as a member of Second Presbyterian Church in Nashville, Tennessee, where he is an elder, heads the nurture (education) committee, sings in the choir, and was a youth advisor until he was elected to the session.

His devotion to music led him to Nashville. He had worked and lived in Dallas, New York City, and San Antonio, but wanted to be in the mecca of country music and asked for a transfer to the Tennessee city. Later he decided that "you can't have a career in the corporate world and be a songwriter, both," so, in his late twenties, he resigned. To help pay the bills while breaking into the music field, he took a job selling shoes—later changing jobs to become a fund raiser for the nonprofit Junior Achievement program—so that "I can have more free time."

What kind of songs does he write? "About fifty percent country, fifty percent popular, although it's highly unlikely that popular songs will be picked up in Nashville because Nashville is country based. Although, country music is becoming more like pop, and pop more like country."

He writes both words and music, and gets ideas from varied sources. "Some from experiences of growing up, and family and friends. Lots of what I write, I see happening to friends. A lot of it is reflective: where are we as a country, and where are we bound?

"I think my No. 1 goal is not to be destructive with the craft. It's easy to fall into negativism, because that sells well. I try to write from a positive perspective."

How much has he sold? A quick laugh, and "Nothing. I've learned that success in the music business involves a lot of politics. Being connected, the right place at the right time is important.

"I've been told the average break-in time is seven or eight years.

"It comes down to the 'is it worth it?' question: Is what you want important enough to put up with the structure that's in place, a system which none of us likes?"

Meanwhile he finds much satisfaction in his church life, and much to be enthusiastic about.

He had "shopped around for a church when I moved here," and found Second Presbyterian to be "a very different place from big churches, one that has a real family feel about it. . . . The congregation is economically very diverse, and with differing theological views; but we can set aside our differences and work together."

Its membership is growing rapidly, he reports. "Seems like we have somebody joining every week or every other week. Eighty families have joined in the past three years. They usually have young children. It may be that everybody is yearning to come to a smaller place; there's something about the way this church incorporates children into its life that I've never seen before.

"This church preaches a lot about real life. There are lots of things that will make you say, "Hmmm." I wonder if there's any other church that has vacation Bible school for the whole family—adults and children, doing things."

He is, not surprisingly, also a fan of Presbyterianism.

"Overall, Presbyterians have been a moderate people, not afraid to be thinking people, not afraid to question. I feel a greater sense of empowerment of the laity.

"The Presbyterian faith, I think, does a great job of bringing everybody into the process. Everyone has a place to play in the ball game.

"I can't even imagine being Presbyterian and not believing in a God who expects you to think for yourself. With thinking for yourself comes a lot of freedom, but a lot of responsibility at the same time."

During and immediately after college he was not active in the church "for about seven years. And I just began missing it."

"One of the things I wish could be addressed more," he adds, has to do with people dropping out of the church. "The reason for this 'jumping-ship', not going to the Presbyterian church, or wherever. It's this feeling that 'life has grown so complicated, and there's so much going on that I feel overwhelmed. And the church has become so complicated, so I'm just going to get back to the basics, back to the Bible.'

"That's people striving for a nice simple life. Unfortunately, I don't think life's going to get any more simple.

❦ Ted Filipi

"When people ask me if I've been born again as a Christian," declares Theodore Anton Filipi, "my answer is always 'Of course not! I've always been!'"

His reaction to the question comes for good reason. The roots of his faith run deep in the rich Nebraska soil, where Czech Presbyterians were among the pioneers who settled in the area in the late 1860s. His father, an immigrant from Czechoslovakia, was a minister in Nebraska for more than 40 years. His late wife's grandfather, though not a clergyman, frequently conducted worship services for the settlers. And her father gave two acres of land as a site for the rural Zion Presbyterian Church, built a bit more than a century ago, about sixty miles northwest of Omaha.

Baptized Bohdan Filipi, but most often known now as Bodie or Ted, Mr. Filipi is steeped in the history of his Czech Presbyterian ancestors and their contributions to the faith.

His father was a divinity student in New York when, at the urging of the Reverend Vaclav Losa, he took a train to Clarkson, Nebraska to serve people in the then-isolated Burwell area. As Ted said not long ago in a speech on the Czech Presbyterian pioneers of the area, "The Reverend Losa met Pa at the depot and took him to the Josef Novotny farm where he had his first meal since leaving New York; all he had had on his three-day trip was fifteen cents worth of rolls he'd bought in Chicago. Little did he envision that in 1927 his son, Bodie, would marry the Novotny daughter, Olga."

In Burwell Ted's father lived in a sod house, preached in a schoolhouse, and conducted his first funeral service for which he received $2.00.

Later the elder Filipi was called to serve in Omaha, again to continue serving the Czech people of the Bohemina Brethren Church.. "My dad served very usefully in Omaha," Ted says. "When people came from Bohemia (now Czechoslovakia) they were told to go up to Filipi's. They would, and my mother gave them supper.

Dad would take them out to get jobs—he had good connections—with the smelter, the railroad shops, the packing houses. They were good workers. And because of the Bohemian Brethren Presbyterian Church of Omaha, the descendants of those people now are doing good as community leaders."

Ted entered the University of Nebraska in 1922, was graduated in 1926, and took a job in New York as a mechanical engineer. The 1929 stock market crash and the subsequent Great Depression cost him his job there. He returned to Nebraska, found that the state needed an engineer, and got the position. By the time he retired in 1972 he was director of the Nebraska Department of Environmental Health. Of his career in that field he says:

"In my thirty-five years I was in every town and village of Nebraska to work for better environment. We put in sewage systems, water supplies, got swimming pools to the point where the water in them could be drunk. We never went to court to get things done; we just reasoned it out. When I left I felt quite comfortable about the health environment of Nebraska."

His church participation has been as constant and as thorough. He has held every office in the First Presbyterian Church of Lincoln—deacon, trustee, elder. He had special talent in the solving of thorny problems, and consequently was appointed to a commission to assist in handling some troubles in another congregation. His reaction now: "I was very humble and proud to be able to help work it out." He has been a commissioner to presbytery and was on a committee for equal representation. His one regret about his years of church work is that he has never been a commissioner to a General Assembly.*

"Now I have the great pleasure of being a handy man. When anything at the church breaks, they call and say, 'Ted, are you coming down?' I come down and fix whatever it is; it's a great privilege and a lot of fun."

Ted doesn't keep up much with the doings of the national church. He "reads with interest all the comments that come out," he reports, but adds that he has "never heard of" the *News of the Presbyterian Church* newspaper, and draws an equal blank on *Presbyterian Survey,* the church's national general interest magazine.

Does that mean the church has a communication problem? "You're right about that. Upstairs, they're doing a lot that the common people don't know about. The roof leaks, but I don't know how to fix it."

From the vantage point of his heritage and a lifetime's participation, what does he see in the church's future? He answers quickly, "We're going to have to put on a big campaign that this is the church of Jesus Christ and not the church of individual people."

What should the church of Jesus Christ do? "First, it's your responsibility to be in church, regardless of who's preaching. Second—a hard job—is to get persons interested in the church, other than the 30 percent who are really active. One year, after Easter we made a concentrated effort to get people to come to church at least once during Pentecost. In the whole program we got 74 percent; 26 percent never came . . . I do believe we ought to have a study made (of other churches) that are taking our members. Unless we have that we don't know why they are growing in strength."

Should Presbyterians concentrate on saving souls, or on such work as feeding the hungry and housing the homeless?

"No question. The answer is yes; but how?

"I think the Presbyterian church has got a big job to do in strengthening the family. By that I mean, too many youngsters are latchkey children. Children in nurseries don't have the same environment they would at home. I'm not liked for what I say, but I think they should have their mamas at home if at all possible."

Ted travels considerably and his itinerary includes frequent visits to Czechoslovakia. Of those trips, he says, "When I get back I offer a long prayer of thanks that my father elected to come to America."

When he was working, Mrs. Filipi went with him as often as possible on the wide-ranging trips that his job sometimes involved. For a variety of reasons, though, they never got to go together to Alaska and Hawaii, two of their big travel goals.

He remembers sadly: "I lost her in 1985 after 57 years . . . Take all those trips while you're together. You just don't know how lonely it is when you're alone."

Then the sad look is replaced by one of wonder as he reflects on the sights they did see together: "I still don't see how God created all these things. It's beyond conception, all the beauty there is in this world."

*National policy-making body of the Presbyterian Church (U.S.A.).

The First Presbyterian Church of Lincoln has 1,109 members. Its pastor is the Reverend Thomas H. Schmid.

❦ *David Welch*

David Welch was a journalism major at the University of Oklahoma when his home church decided to sponsor a young person as a participant in a summer work group in southern Africa.

"A lot of us applied," he recalls, "and they picked me to go. I had a wonderful time. It changed my life drastically.

"I lived without electricity or running water in the home where I stayed. That kind of brought me down to realizing all the benefits we live with here and the easy life we have. I saw people there with subsistence living, and being very happy—people living in small homes with thatched mud roofs and walls. I was greatly impressed by their endurance and tenacity, their resourcefulness. So when I came back to the States I was really culture shocked. I decided that getting caught in the rat race of careers and lifestyles here, in lives full of competing for money and materialism, did not please me any more."

David is a member of the First Presbyterian Church of

Tulsa, and the trip that so affected him was a project of the Medical Benevolence Foundation, a Presbyterian-related group that focuses on medical mission work abroad.

After his first trip, he says, "I came back and reported to my church, and they were really happy with the experience I'd had and the work we'd accomplished. They decided to keep on with the program of sending people over there."

Consequently he has been to southern Africa twice more, working in Zambia, Malawi, Botswana, and Zimbabwe. "Each time I had different experiences, but they're all similar."

He began thinking about how to spend his life—"trying to figure out what I could do to help other people, to make life a little easier—so I decided anthropology was the way to go because it is mainly the study of human beings and how they adapt to the environment they live in.

"I really wanted to focus my life on what I could do to benefit other people's lives instead of just becoming a participant in life. At that time, in the mid and late '80s when materialism was at a high point in American culture, I really wanted to take a step back from that and re-evaluate my values—which placed me in a spot where I didn't really need what a lot of Americans wanted. At the time I wanted to go back to Africa and work there in mission hospitals, because I saw the work we did there materialize right in front of us.

"My parents and my family, being a large family and a tight-knit group, wanted me to stay here in the States. So I tried to refocus those needs to help; I thought I'd redirect that and work here in the States.

Meantime David finished his undergraduate studies at the University of Oklahoma, with a degree in anthropology and a minor in history. In 1992 he was a member of the college staff at Ghost Ranch, a Presbyterian study center in northern New Mexico; at the end of the summer got an ongoing job there "doing environmental control, if that's what you want to call it." His duties: "Do the garbage and recycling, and also work in the anthropology museum; I'm also on the maintenance crew as well, so my time's split up."

But mainly, "It's really nice because I get to learn about the cultures here, and the people in the area, the different communities around Ghost Ranch. I'll get some time to pick up all kinds of experiences that will help me on my path."

David is the youngest of five brothers. "My family is Presbyterian, so I was raised in the Presbyterian church."

Although "I haven't been a church-going person in college, being Presbyterian kind of gave me a foundation on which I built, in my college years."

For one thing, "I noticed that out here, where Presbyterians have been, the first thing they do is build a school, they build a hospital or a clinic, and they do these before they go in and build a church or a religious institution. I agree with those values of a medical ministry, and education. So I think that's where the Presbyterian church has made an impact on me, putting lots of emphasis on those two ideals."

He sees the church in his future, as well. "Somehow I'll always be a Presbyterian, always be going to Presbyterian churches, I'm sure. At one time I thought about going into the ministry, but I didn't think I could impact people's lives the way I wanted to. I can see myself in the role almost of a social worker, being a communicator between these people and the Presbyterian church, with education and medical needs, just basically Presbyterian outreach."

He believes the church has major responsibilities in the teaching and healing of the future, as well:

"I think the church is going to have to help with health care that involves setting up clinics in small towns across the country. And by doing that in other countries that are less fortunate. It seems that the need for a good health care plan for others, and in our country, is inevitable. I think it's really the key, that and education."

As an anthropologist is he optimistic about the future of the Earth?

"I am. Very optimistic. We have all the tools we need in front of us. It's just a matter of people using these tools to make our country work right. I see our country as a leader in energy efficiency; I think that's going to be a key to life. Basically we're going to have to realize that we all live on one planet, on planet Earth, and that all humans on Earth are going to have to work together so that it doesn't become one large landfill."

The First Presbyterian Church of Tulsa has 2,520 members. Its interim pastor is the Reverend James D. Miller.

❦ *Gordon Stewart*

In some summer times between his study times at Maryville College in Tennessee, Gordon Stewart worked in a street social work program in a Philadelphia ghetto. The experience changed his life.

Actually there had been some life-shaping events earlier, but none so sharply-etched. The son of a Presbyterian minister, he had always said "No" to enquiries about following in his father's footsteps: "It never occurred to me that I would ever be a minister. I always thought it was an inappropriate question."

However, at a summer camp between his junior and senior years in high school, "There was a pastor named John Rowland who spoke to senior highs. He gathered us all up and put us in a meeting room to talk to us about church vocations. I just ran for cover. I figured everybody knew I was a preacher's kid and would put the finger on me. I put myself in the back row, right in the corner, as far away from that guy as I could get, and out of sight.

"But he talked to us about Christian vocations; he said that every Christian had a vocation and that within that vocation some had the vocation of the ministry of word and sacrament. He told us to ask ourselves the question of whether God might be calling us to a church vocation. For the first time in my life, ever, it became an objective question. It was just like a light dawning, and I started asking myself the question.

"At that point I wanted to do missionary work. I was another kid with stars in my eyes; I was going to save the world. I went to Maryville with that intent."

Then came the ghetto experience. "I was working with kids, playing dodge ball, in the streets. The ball went down this one-block-long street, and I had to go get it.

"There was this group of men we then called winos; in the middle of the afternoon they would haul the jug out. And I had to go through a group of those guys to retrieve the ball.

"They wanted to know what I was doing there, and I told them that the program was to give the kids something to do. I was shaking in my boots, but they only asked, 'Do you have any games for us?'

"So I got quoits and took them out on the street, and we would play quoits every afternoon.

"On my last day with those guys, they sat me down and said, 'This is your last day and we've got some things we want to say to you. We want to say thanks for being with us; but you're going back to your college and we're staying here. If you want to help us, you go back and tell your people in the suburbs that things aren't going to change for us until they change out there; because it's people in your church who own our tenements; they own our buildings and they won't fix the plumbing. They won't fix this, won't do that.'

"And they went right on down the list: 'They own the ghetto.' Bells went off all over the place in my head."

He gave up studying sociology "because it was so boring and bore so little resemblance to actual social reality. I ended up in philosophy and majored in political science."

There were other formative experiences for young Gordon Stewart. "I took a course in existentialism and contemporary philosophy that rocked my faith to the core; I spent most of my time reading philosophy and trying to make sense of my life." A couple of teachers at Maryville "helped me put it back together" when he monitored a course for pastors on contemporary theology. "It turned me around, so I had a choice to make between going on to Ph.D. work in philosophy, or going to McCormick Seminary. I decided on seminary, and on McCormick because it was urban, and because it was focused on the city."

He considered graduate school after seminary, as preparation for a career in teaching but, thinking it over while recovering from mononucleosis, "I decided that all that philosophy business didn't make any sense unless it was rooted in life and death issues, and I'd been hanging around ivory towers long enough."

After seminary graduation he went to the First Presbyterian Church of Decatur, Illinois as an assistant pastor responsible for adult education.

"Those were the days of Harvey Cox's *Secular City* and the Kerner Report (on racism and police violence). The Decatur church went into a program with OEO (Office of Economic Opportunity) for kids living in housing projects; I was responsible for the program, along with the OEO person. We had about one thousand kids enrolled.

"I stood in the middle of riots three different times in Decatur.

"I left there two and a half years later, to do campus ministry for United Ministries in Higher Education in Whitewater,Wisconsin. I can't even begin to tell you about all of that. There was the celebrated Whitewater Four case; we campus ministers were involved in that: a group of professors who had been summarily suspended from their university for (allegedly) provoking riots.

"It had started with a basketball game and wound up in a white fraternity house where a gun was fired four times. By the time I arrived on my job a month or so later they had charged 18 black students—and no white students—and had moved the hearing to a courthouse in the county seat 12 miles away and didn't even offer transportation to the black kids. They had no cars, so we transported them.

"We actually came up with a solution between the fraternity leaders and the black community, which was sabotaged by the college administration.They wanted to hang them out to dry, and that's what they did."

Years passed, and Gordon Stewart found himself in a different kind of touchy situation in the summer of 1991. He had moved on from strictly campus ministry to the pastorate of a congregation on campus in Wooster, Ohio, and about six years later to Cincinnati and the pastorate of the Knox Presbyterian Church there. And to a role as a commissioner in the Presbyterian General Assembly, where he headed a committee dealing with a highly controversial report on human sexuality.

Recommendations growing out of a lengthy study were to be presented: recommendations that had stirred a whirlwind of counter recommendations. The committee headed by Stewart had to deal with them in a fishbowl of publicity and controversy.

He was widely praised for the compassionate and evenhandedness of his work in and with the committee, and in plenary sessions of six hundred-plus voting delegates from throughout the country.

In the course of his experiences,he gained a wide-screen view of the calling he had earlier thought to avoid, and of the denomination in which he is a minister.

"I think there's an exciting future," he says of the Presbyterian Church (U.S.A.), "if we get it straight. I grieve over lots of what I see, but there's also a lot to celebrate.

"What has happened over the last decade is that we've lost the sense of ourselves as a family, beyond the local community. We don't even have much of a sense of it in the city; we think of ourselves as congregations. And frankly, I lay that on the doorstep of us pastors; we see ourselves too parochially.

"But the thing to celebrate is that there's a tremendous ministry being done in those congregations: the grassroots responding to needs, wanting to be involved in real ministry rather than sending money off to someone else.

"The job is to reestablish trust and mutual understanding, between people in our congregations and people who serve the church at the General Assembly, synod, and presbytery. I think the day is really gone when the General Assembly has the ability to tell any Presbyterian much of anything—because people are not in the mood to be told anything, by anybody, unless they ask first. And I don't hear too many people in the pews asking the General Assembly about how to live their lives, one way or the other.

"The local church, it seems to me, has a perception of what's going on that is at least a couple of years, if not five to ten, behind what the reality is at the General Assembly level. What I see by and large at the Assembly is people who are working very hard, who struggle with very few resources, because the congregations have made it so and the presbyteries have kept more for themselves. But good people are working very hard, trying to keep their chins up when they are perceived as the bad guys. And I think that can be turned around. I don't think it takes a lot; it's not that complicated. What we need is more eyeball-to-eyeball conversation. Less perception of the General Assembly as a governing body or a staff which is the only prophet of God, and is more with folks as far as possible—with a human face, and which listens before it speaks.

"If we can do that, have real conversation between the General Assembly, presbyteries, synods, and the ordinary folks who are doing ministry in our own communities, it'll turn around. With great energy, and with some fire in our bones, because of what God has called us to do.

"So we've got to get off the name calling, the labels; to leave the old agendas. They don't work any more. They're all out of date.

"The kind of polarization we saw leading up to the 1991 General Assembly need not happen that way. We need to back off and listen.

"We live in such a time of change that we need to listen

to the Spirit a whole lot more than we do. We would do well to shut up for a while and listen. That's at all levels of the church."

Does Gordon Stewart think, then, that the church is going to survive?

"Sure I do. Part of the problem is that we keep asking that question. The church is going to survive whether we do or not. We have a survival mentality, but that's not where my church, my congregation, is. The congregation is thriving. So far this year we've received forty-seven new members, got a new member class that will probably be between thrity and forty. So by the fifth month of the year we'll probably have received seventy-five to eighty-five people. That's because the people in the church reach out to those who come in.

"When the church is serious about what it is called to be and do, it's not going to die. We've got to take seriously as a church the age in which we live, and come to grips with problems of the claims of the uniqueness of Christ in a religiously plural world. . . .

"That's the long-haul issue. The key to the future of the Presbyterian church, in my judgment, is that we have to reclaim the Reformed tradition. I don't mean Calvinism, don't mean closed arteries of the post-reformation period. I mean the reformation period of the church always reformed and always re-forming. We have to start sending seminarians to Presbyterian seminaries, have to insist that they go to those seminaries.

"We've got a real problem with the quality of ministry—a serious, serious problem. Our presbytery has taken a position that (if you want to be a Presbyterian minister) you will go to a Presbyterian seminary, period, unless you can show compelling reasons for an exception.

"One thing we have to do is reclaim the Reformed tradition. The other is to be open and responsive to the world around us; living as though we do in fact live by grace. We have to start living in grace, and stop living in fear."

Gordon Stewart is now pastor of Westminster Presbyterian Church in Minneapolis.

❦ *Margaret Towner*

Margaret Towner posed a bit of a puzzle when she went to her first presbytery meeting after being ordained to the gospel ministry.

She was the first woman so ordained—the first woman minister in the Presbyterian church. "They didn't know what to do with me," she recalls. "Here they had a woman, and the form of address for commissioners to presbytery in those days was 'fathers and brethren.' The moderator of presbytery was a man, of course, as were most of the others. There were women elders, but not a lot. Finally the moderator said, 'Well, I don't know; we've got a problem. What do we do, how do we address the presbytery—brethren and sistern?'"

That was in 1956. The General Assembly of the Presbyterian Church in the United States of America* had voted in 1955 to ordain women to the ministry, and the vote was ratified by its presbyteries in the twelve months following, with the final approving action taken at the following General Assembly.

Margaret was not at the 1956 General Assembly—"I was quite involved in the church I was serving, in Allentown, Pennsylvania"—but she recalls some of the details pertaining to the landmark decision.

"Lillian Alexander, a ruling elder, recommended that Rochester Presbytery send an overture to the '55 Assembly. I don't remember now whether I was at the Lehigh Presbytery meeting when they voted on concurring, but the final presbyteries' vote wasn't close. A few voted negatively.

"There weren't many women eligible for ordination at the time. Pat Chaplin, Margaret Howland, Marideen Visscher, and I think Pat Keppler. I really didn't know I was going to be the first; in fact I was sure someone would have been ordained between May and October, so it hadn't crossed my mind."

A couple of incidents related to her ordination still bring chuckles to the now-retired Margaret Towner.

"I really wasn't sure how I came to be ordained as early as I was, but this is the story I was told:

"It seems that my home pastor, Bill McConaghy, and Richard Firth, who was in Syracuse, played golf a lot with Arthur Mielke. (Art was pastor of Park Central Presbyterian Church in Syracuse at the time, and quite influential). Dick told me that the topic of conversation that pretty much preoccupied them all summer in their golf games was 'How do we go about getting Marg Towner ordained?' Dick said, 'Let's get Art Mielke out on the golf course and see if we can talk him into it.' So they arranged the game, and before they teed off Bill took Dick off to the side and said, 'let Art win.'"

Her home presbytery was Cayuga–Syracuse, in upstate New York. Her first job after graduation from Union (New York) Theological Seminary was as director of Christian education at the Takoma Park (Maryland) Presbyterian Church, and she was in charge of Christian education in the First Presbyterian Church of Allentown when ordination became a possibility. The pastor of First Presbyterian in Syracuse—her home church—invited her to consider being ordained there and her colleagues in Allentown agreed.

"The big to-do was the process whereby I was transferred to Cayuga–Syracuse for ordination, then transferred back to Lehigh for membership, and there was a little bit of a technical hassle over how to accomplish that. I was a member of Lehigh Presbytery as a commissioned church worker and would have to be transferred to Cayuga–Syracuse in that status, and immediately back to Lehigh as a minister of Word and Sacrament. But Gene Blake (Eugene Carson Blake, at that time the stated clerk of the General Assembly) and the stated clerks of the two presbyteries straightened out the mechanics of it all."

Born in Columbia, Missouri, the daughter of a Presbyterian minister, Margaret went to Carleton College and got extensive training in photography along with her Bachelor of Arts degree. She worked in the medical photography department at the Mayo clinic, had her own studio, and as the thesis for her Master of Divinity degree at Union made a film for the 1954 national meeting of Presbyterian Women.

"So I was really honored when *Life* magazine sent Alfred Eisenstadt, the great photographer, to cover my ordination. My mother invited him to come to our house for reception and supper, and it was fun to get to know him. He was so skillful at getting pictures that people didn't even realize he was around. At the ceremonies and back in Allentown, he took more then 300 pictures—of which *Life* printed eight or 10."

Once she decided on the ministry, it was the center of her life. "I chose not to be married. I felt strongly called to my vocation in ministry, and I realized early on that I couldn't have handled both that vocation and marriage. So I made a rather deliberate choice.

"After the stories about my ordination hit the news media around the country (and world, for that matter), I received a number of proposals of marriage from conservative males who offered to marry me 'to get me out of my predicament,' referring to my sinning against the Bible (in their view) by being ordained. They even sent their pictures.

"By and large, though, most of my mail was very supportive of my ordination and some of it even reunited me with long lost friends, male and female, from elementary and high school years."

"I felt very definitely called to ministry. Whenever I had tried some other vocation, doors closed; but they opened to me when I entered the ministry of Word and Sacrament. I think God calls us to vocations, and calls men and women to ministry."

Her ministry has included pastoral or education work in Syracuse, New York; Allentown Pennsylvania; Takoma Park, Maryland; Kalamazoo, Michigan; Indianapolis, Indiana, and from 1973 to her retirement in 1990, as a co-pastor in the six-church Kettle Moraine Parish in Waukesha County, Wisconsin. She has been vice moderator of the General Assembly (in 1981), and on top-level councils and committees dealing with policy, worship, administration, education, vocation, and more. One of her most recent involvements has been membership on a national committee studying the denomination's system of governance, and recommending ways to improve it.

From the beginning, she has taken a quiet but determined path in her pioneering role as the denomination's first clergywoman.

"I guess I was a little numb, at first. I turned down a lot of invitations to go places and speak, because it would mean being away from the job. I did accept some that were close by, so I could get to them and get back to Allentown without losing any work time.

"I did quietly keep working toward getting people to accept women in ministry. At first I did it rather unobtrusively. I didn't get out on a soap box; I felt that what was needed was a rather gentle approach to breaking down barriers. It was only in later years that I became more aggressive, such as when I was chair of a committee dealing with language about God. I felt first of all we had to earn acceptance and credibility, and as more and more women were ordained, let them speak out more and more forcefully. Some women got angry; I didn't feel that was appropriate."

But being gentle didn't mean accepting second-class status.

"Early on, there was a lot of patronizing. There was a group of ministers who met, I think it was monthly, for an afternoon and an evening. In the afternoon they would study a paper that one of the pastors had prepared. The wives would be excluded from the discussion, and could only join in for supper and after.

"When I was ordained I wasn't too happy with the idea of sitting and knitting; I wanted to be involved in the discussion. It happened that the wife of one of the ministers was a woman who had been a professor of Christian education at Princeton; we insisted on being part of the discussion, and had the support of her husband. So we finally became part of the discussion group, and not the sewing and knitting group.

"But generally, there was great acceptance and I was very active in presbytery, especially in education and youth work, and in the synod."

She is encouraged by the advancements women have made—"for example, from what I have seen and heard, women seminarians are walking away with many of the preaching and theology prizes." But that is not to say all the problems of women in ministry have been solved.

"One of the fears expressed when I was ordained was that women would become threats to the job security of male clergy. What I'm hearing now is a greater feeling of that threat. There is still discrimination out there—a lot of people who are still enamored with the literal translation of Paul's epistles.

"Part of it is a cultural problem, a sort of backlash against women's rights and equality. I think what I'm seeing is the condition of the church as a mirror of culture. I attribute it to the ultra conservatism of the Reagan years, making it more difficult for women in ministry and in law and other disciplines, to be accepted as equal partners.

"I hope this, too, will pass. My dream is that we will come to a time in our world when we can somehow get rid of sexual stereotyping, and women and men can work together as colleagues, as people who are equals."

* The Presbyterian Church in the United States of America was the largest of three branches of the denomination in this country at that time. It merged with the United Presbyterian Church of North America in 1958, forming the United Presbyterian Church in the United States of America. This group and the Presbyterian Church in the United States were reunited in 1983, forming the present Presbyterian Church (U.S.A.).

❦ *Christy Sackett*

Some of the things Christy Sackett does for the church she belongs to are these: She is moderator of the Board of Deacons, teaches a Sunday school class and prepares the monthly newsletter. The deacons of the Montezuma Valley Presbyterian Church in Cortez, Colorado, make preparations for Communion services, for coffee fellowship time, for potluck suppers on third Sundays during the school year, and for a variety of other congregational events. She was a member of the pastor nominating committee that recommended the Reverend Malcolm McQueen as the church's present pastor.

Christy Sackett says candidly, "I'm not really interested in anything beyond the local church; I'm not interested in the politics. I belong to the church because of God. I can go there for peace and quiet, and it's just Him and me."

Her daughter, Megan, age 11, is involved along with her mother in church activities. She sings in the adult choir, plays in the handbell choir and, her mother adds, "loves the

Logos (a study/activities plan for children and youth) program.

"We have our Sunday mornings sometimes when Megan doesn't feel like going, but she's not afraid at this age to admit to other people that she goes to church."

Church activities aren't just something to fill the day for Christy. She is a single parent who works 50 hours or so a week in her job as a newspaper production manager, in addition to the time that being a mother requires. So the question occurs, what does the church do for her?

"I know I can go there and I will not find enemy one," she quickly replies.

"We're all a large family. They have just been part of my life. They didn't shun me when I got my divorce. They stood behind me. They've been with my parents when my brother had a kidney transplant (Christy donated the needed kidney). It's a feeling of their just being there."

She was born in Kansas. Her family moved to Cortez when Christy was in the third grade and she has lived there ever since. "My father was born and raised here; my mother came from Kansas. We've always been Presbyterians."

The congregation seems to be growing, she observes, "Especially with children and younger people. We're headed for more growth, for learning more. This has been a quiet church, but we've become more involved in ecumenical things in the last few years. And we're becoming more involved in the community; reaching out to those who are churchless. An evangelism program is getting started."

As for money, "As far as I know we're down, but I have a feeling that's just in the past year, because of the economy. The economy of Cortez is not the greatest. But we have a church with a lot of members who are really good when it comes to donations.

"Where we're headed right now is what I'm happy with. When I was growing up in the church there were a lot of young people. The church seemed to have lost a lot of youth for a while, but in the past three or four years we're beginning to have more. We're still a church getting more young people, I think."

The need to attract young people was on the minds of the pastor nominating committee members, she says. "One of the things we discussed in the committee was "to look for a younger pastor." But there was much more to the work of the committee than that.

"At first I wasn't confident that I could do a good enough job for the committee. You sometimes wondered if all that paperwork was necessary but in the long run it was helpful, both to the committee and the minister. I think it (particularly the church information form) is helpful to do every once in a while, even if you're not looking for a pastor. It helps congregations to see where they're failing, where they can improve."

Going through the forms and formalities of searching for a pastor "was a long eighteen months," she adds, "but it was worth the wait."

If Christy Sackett could send a message to the rest of the Presbyterian Church (U.S.A.), what would she say?

"I'd say we need to focus on the real reason why we're Presbyterians. The real reason I'm Presbyterian is that I'm not pressured on what to believe. If I say, 'This is the way I interpret this,' nobody's going to tell me I'm wrong.

"Like I said before, it's between God and me. I know He's there. He knows I'm here. It's between Him and me."

The Montezuma Valley Presbyterian Church of Cortez, Colorado, has 208 members. Its pastor is the Reverend Malcolm L. McQueen.

Clarence Cave ❦

Clarence Cave is involved in a project that is due for completion in 2007. In a sense the undertaking was launched in 1981. In a more crucial sense it dates to 1807—the year when black Presbyterianism took on a congregational life of its own.

What Clarence Cave is doing—as need dictates—is being chairperson, editor, or project director of a publication named *Periscope*. It is intended that an issue of *Periscope* appear every five years, the final issue coinciding with the bicentennial of the world's first African American Presbyterian church.

It's appropriate that this slim, intense man is spending time on the project, inasmuch as he has been much involved in the life of the congregation, fittingly named the First African Presbyterian Church, in Philadelphia. He was parish associate (a minister assisting in the life of a congregation, although not on its paid staff) from 1979 to 1989. And he was involved for much of his professional career in working for the rights of African American Presbyterians.

Clarence had retired from his salaried work a year before he left his volunteer's post at First African, forty-one years after being ordained to the ministry.

"I had never had any desire to become a minister," he said, before his path crossed that of Edler G. Hawkins. Mr. Hawkins, who later would become the first black moderator of the United Presbyterian General Assembly, also became a lifelong hero and role model for young Cave.

He was in a special school (Stuyvesant High School in New York City, a school with high academic requirements) and wanted to be a medical doctor. "Then here came Edler Hawkins and I saw something altogether different from what I knew." The course of his life was never really in doubt after that.

Finishing high school, he enrolled in City College of New York and was planning to move on to seminary when the United States got into World War II. Classified 1-A, he appeared to be headed for the military instead. But the National Council of Churches "noticed that Roman Catholic students studying for the ministry were routinely getting deferred, and took up the cause of Protestants." As a result his classification was changed from 1-A to 4-D, he was graduated from CCNY in 1944 and from Union (New York) Seminary in 1947.

He was ordained immediately after seminary, and accepted an offer to do urban church work for the denomination's Board of National Missions.

"The presbytery's committee related to my work called me in after ten months in the field to review my activities with the youth and young people. Hearing that I was using homes for meetings, rather than the woefully inadequate, deteriorating facilities of the church, the chairperson was outraged. When I suggested to him that this practice was consistent with my knowledge of the New Testament, he called me a 'smart alec,' ended the meeting, contacted the board, and recommended my immediate withdrawal from Denver and my job terminated."

He was not thrown out, but reassigned to Philadelphia

and New York. In 1950 he received a call to be pastor of the Faith Presbyterian Church in the Germantown section of the Philadelphia area.

"This was my first and only pastorate. During the course of my thirteen years there, the church doubled in membership, and attracted several professionally trained young adults who gave active leadership to community concerns. And it gained a reputation in the Germantown area for its support of the Selective Patronage Program, a city-wide boycott of businesses and industries by four hundred Black pastors and congregations, under the leadership of the Reverend Leon Sullivan. The objective, of course, was to secure job opportunities for Blacks and to end segregation practices in the work place."

The denomination's Board of Christian Education asked him to join its staff in 1963, when mainline religious groups were getting more and more involved in civil rights activities. He began with the board in its Church and Society division. "My assignment was economic issues, for which I was poorly prepared," he says candidly. "If I were grading my work in that field, I would give myself a 'C'."

Shortly thereafter he was given a new assignment, racial affairs, "And that was a different ball of wax! I became a member of an inter-agency staff group called the National Race Staff, headed by the Reverend Gayraud S. Wilmore, Jr., who had earlier taken a leave of absence from the faculty of Pittsburgh Theological Seminary to direct the United Presbyterian Church's new Commission on Religion and Race.

"With the restructuring of the General Assembly agencies in the early 1970s, several of my colleagues including Earl Larson, Oscar McCloud, Robert Newbold, Gayraud Wilmore, and Donald Wilson, continued their labors in other areas of ministry."

Clarence Cave makes it clear that an organization known as the Afro-American Presbyterian Council had greatly influenced his mind and spirit in his preparation for ministry.

"Indeed it did! It was there, at the annual meetings of the council, that I came to know something about denominational racism: the 'invisibility' of Black Presbyterians, the demeaning patterns of segregation, the lack of opportunities for ministry other than in the parish, and a pervasive paternalism that hampered respectful race relations.

"But in spite of it all, it was a time of challenge and change, and a new breed of Black clergy was moving into positions of leadership in the council: Edler Hawkins, Robert Johnson, LeRoy Patrick, James Robinson, and others. These men, and women like Thelma Adair and Emily Gibbes, began to set new agendas, new goals, and strategies." The Afro-American Presbyterian Council had been established in 1894; it revised its constitution in 1947, changed its name, opened its membership to all clergy and congregations, and affirmed again its commitment to racial justice and equality.

"To underscore its faith, hope, and confidence in an integrated church, the council dissolved itself in 1957, and turned its modest treasury over to the office of the stated clerk of the General Assembly. It was our way of recognizing Eugene Carson Blake's leadership in the unfolding civil rights struggle.

"We had gotten only a year or two into the sixties when it became apparent there was a need for a small group of lay and clergy people to come together. The nation by then was caught up in a racial crisis, and it was equally clear that we had to act. And we did. We called ourselves Concerned Presbyterians, a 'compact, disciplined, purposeful group' of 30 ministers and laypersons. Bryant George handled coordination and strategy concerns; Edler Hawkins, once known as a troublemaker and later revered for his statesmanlike qualities, managed our church relations; and Gayraud Wilmore edified us with his insights in Christian ethics and social analysis. Their leadership was an act of divine Providence; it kept alive the need of an organized Black presence to be the conscience of our church."

From his perspective as an African American who was in the civil rights struggle for so long, where is the Presbyterian church in terms of civil rights today?

"However you define the current situation, I have no reason to believe that our church has made any headway, or even secured all the gains we made in the sixties and seventies. The reunion of 1983—however much it may have addressed the significance of unity of the church—has given African Americans and other persons of color little reason for rejoicing.

"If recent history is to repeat itself, I do not see black Presbyterians accommodating themselves to a lesser role in the life and witness of the church. On the contrary, we are encouraged by the growing number of women entering the ministry and receiving attention far beyond their parishes. We are encouraged by the growing interest in black worship and preaching, and their implications for evangelism. Not to be overlooked is the encouragement we are getting from the newly merged National Black Presbyterian Caucus and its newly developed goals and priorities for the future."

Speaking of the future, he is reminded of some words written by James Foster Reese in *Periscope 3,* the publication that is getting so much of Clarence Cave's time:

"We are moving toward a century that will be increasingly urbanized, multicultural, and global. Black Presbyterians will arrive there with our heritage, our history, our perspective. The gifts and skills of black Presbyterians will be needed as never before. *Periscope 3* gives us a starting point. The year 2007 awaits our arrival."

Dean and Cindy Pickett
❦

"I think we would be remiss," says Cindy Pickett toward the end of an evening's conversation, "if we didn't mention what has happened in our lives in the past year." She is speaking of a program called "Walk to Emmaus,"* an event that clearly made and is making a notable impact on them. Describing it, she and her husband Dean use words such as "very meaningful, structured, spiritual renewal, truly ecumenical, really targeted for busy people of the 1990s."

It is not a physical walk, the Picketts explain, but rather a spiritual one that starts with a three-day weekend meeting and continues in weekly meetings of small groups of people. The weekend includes worship, prayer, discussion, and singing. While ministers are involved the event, in Dean's words, "It is totally lay-driven, and that is the key to its success."

Husbands do the weekend retreat first, and wives meet for a later weekend. Separate male and female reunion groups of six or so have weekly follow-up meetings in which, Cindy explains, 'We talk about the week, about when we've done something we shouldn't have done, about when we've felt closest to Christ." Prayer and sometimes singing are part of the small group meetings.

The Emmaus Walk "really refocuses you," she adds. "It goes to the Gospel of Luke on how you are walking with Christ. It reaches down in your soul."

Couples sponsor other couples for the initial weekends. Some friends sponsored the Picketts, who have since sponsored another couple.

Dean Pickett is an attorney whose primary work is that of representing Northern Arizona University and several school districts. Cindy is a high-school teacher whose courses include world history, geography, and a reading/writing laboratory.

Although baptized in a Lutheran church as a child, she attended a Presbyterian church most of the time in those years because "it was the closest church with a youth group, so my parents sent my sisters and me there." Dean, also baptized in a Lutheran church, says that "my church attendance was sporadic" during his growing-up years. They met at Northern Arizona University (in Flagstaff), occasionally attending the Federated Community Church there. They joined it after "a little church-shopping" when they moved back to Flagstaff following Navy service and law school.

People from seventeen different denominations are on the rolls of Federated Church and "no one knows who is what," Cindy says. She adds, "The beauty of Federated Church is that it is ecumenical. I don't consider myself truly a Presbyterian any more; I'm really Federated." They estimate that Presbyterians and Methodists make up the largest part, with about 40 percent each. The current pastor, the Reverend Reford Nash, is Presbyterian; Methodist and Presbyterian ministers traditionally alternate in its pastorate.

Both Cindy and Dean have taught Sunday school, but "We're shying away from junior and senior high now because our children are in that age bracket and they get enough of us at home."

Cindy continues, "We have some dynamite youth leaders who have pre-school children, so we take care of their children while they take care of ours. It's just giving back to the system."

Dean: "Our kids fought church for awhile, just as we did, in a sense. But they're finding more of a commitment. It's part of their lives, too."

Cindy: "That's something I look back on in the Presbyterian church when I was growing up. It didn't matter that my parents never put a foot in the Presbyterian sanctuary, I was welcomed for myself." They were not regular churchgoers during the law school years, what with study and work dominating the time of both of them.

Dean: "For me, it was just part of my pattern. I had never been through a confirmation class. We were married right after graduating from college, by an Episcopal priest. I went to Communion in an Episcopal church but I couldn't—wouldn't—participate because I didn't understand it. It was painful. I cried; I sobbed. Then later at a Communion service after I came to understand, I did participate, and I cried again, for joy. I felt accepted, enveloped." (Later, he adds, "In the Walk to Emmaus, everyone was given an opportunity to serve Communion. I felt I had come full circle.")

Both the Picketts are elders and have been on the church's board of trustees. He "reads, religiously, the religion section of the newspaper because I am interested in the politics of religion." They get the *News of the Presbyterian Church* and *The Layman,* "so in that sense we're keeping up" with what happens in the Presbyterian church nationally. "I did some work with the presbytery in a discipline case and another activity, so I identify with the Presbyterian church. One thing that I respect about the church, and which in my mind should keep it healthy and active, is that it can handle such dissent as was stirred over the sexuality report.

"I don't agree with the kind of poison pen approach of *The Layman,* but I think it's healthy that the church can tolerate it.

"Federated Church had a forum in which the issue (of sexuality) could be debated and resolved. I would have still stayed on the Presbyterian rolls at Federated if the decision on the issue had come out the other way."

Cindy adds, "I remember as a youth hearing about the Angela Davis† thing. That sort of pulled me away for a time, but I overcame it."

Both are optimistic about the church but express different reasons for it. Cindy says, "I see a healthy future for Federated Church. For the Presbyterian church in general, I can only speak of what I know well: I think the future is healthy as long as there is a good, strong, youth group. As long as the youth have a good understanding of God and Jesus and the church, how it works and why it works—they may leave for a time, but they will come back."

Dean says, "What we're trying to do with our children is to make clear that work in the church, play in the church, are vital to their lives.

"We're members of what was, ten years ago, being accused of being the 'Me' generation, but I'm hopeful that it's not going to be like that, that the next generation coming up is going to have a broader perspective."

"One of the things that should energize people in the church, in the Presbyterian church, is that we don't have to look to one man in the Vatican; believing Christ is working through a lot of people in a lot of ways, we may not always agree with each other but we can stay together. How remarkably similar to the U.S. Constitution is our *Book of Order*. This is a church that has a foundation to grow and evolve and still meet the needs of Christians."

---

* The Walk to Emmaus program began as the "Cursillo" in Spain in the 1940s and came to America a decade later. It was primarily a Roman Catholic movement until the 1970s. The Upper Room (United Methodist) is a major sponsor. A similar program, called Chrysalis, is for 15- to 22-year-olds.

† In 1971, a grant of $10,000 was made from the former United Presbyterian Church's Legal Defense Fund for the defense of Angela Davis, an African American and self-described Communist who was accused in a California murder case. The contribution stirred a national controversy; ten

African American members of the denomination subsequently gave $1,000 each to the fund in response to the backlash. Ms. Davis was eventually acquitted of all charges.

The Federated Community Church of Flagstaff has 620 members and divides its funds among Presbyterian and United Methodist causes.

Fred Heuser 🍂

One day in 1982 Lorraine Heuser saw a job advertisement on a bulletin board at Drexel University in Philadelphia, where she was working. She told her husband about it, and he applied for the post. A short time later he was invited to an interview and, he remembers, "Bill Miller said, 'You're the person I want for the job.'"

William B. Miller was director of the Presbyterian Historical Society, and he hired Frederick J. Heuser as an assistant archivist there. Eight years later Bill Miller had retired and Fred Heuser, who had received two promotions in the meantime, was elected to succeed him.

"I've had a pretty strong sense that this was where I wanted to be, where God wanted me," Fred Heuser says now. "In retrospect, all my education and work experience prepared me for this. It's a tremendously satisfying experience."

He has been interested in history longer than he has been a Presbyterian. He earned a Bachelor of Arts degree from Rider College, Lawrenceville, New Jersey, in history, and taught history at the same time he was working toward a master's in European history at Villanova University outside Philadelphia. In 1991 he earned a Ph.D. in history, at Villanova.

"Then I had decided I didn't want to teach, so I got a master's in library science at Drexel, with concentration on archives." He was working in the New Jersey state archives in Trenton when the Historical Society job came to his attention.

Born in Philadelphia to Roman Catholic parents, he spent eight years in Catholic schools and "worshiped in a Roman Catholic Church, not because I wanted to but because I felt I had to." He dropped out of that church while in college, over differences associated with the Vietnam War: "I couldn't agree with priests who told me I should kill people" in that conflict.

He and Lorraine were married in a Methodist Church. They "began looking for a church to join in the late 1970s, and one day around 1982 we stumbled into a Presbyterian Church in Collingswood, New Jersey. We liked it, and became active. We've done the typical things—deacons, elder, vacation church school."

He says, "I think I was probably always a Presbyterian at heart. I had trouble with Catholic views on authority, and the Presbyterian church for me has always been a thinking people's church; there's no final earthly authority."

He found Presbyterian positions on a number of social issues in agreement with his own, "but it was my longing to be part of a faith community that brought me to be Presbyterian."

Where, from a historian's vantage point, does he see the Presbyterian church going?

"It's anybody's guess, but I think there'll be a smaller national structure, probably more efficient, more limited in scope. And working in tandem with the presbyteries on mission projects.

"In the nineteenth century the church didn't really have a national bureaucracy, except for the foreign mission operation that was established in 1837. The rest didn't come until later. The national mission board officially started in 1924, although there had been a home mission group that was organized in 1878 (the Women's Board of Home Missions) and basically worked with the presbyteries.

"There's more of a shift back to the presbyteries. People are concerned about their own regions; that's where they feel they can have an impact."

He has "a strong suspicion" that there will be similar geographical changes in the centers of action in other mainline denominations, and believes this "will put more of a burden on local mainline churches toward cooperating with non-mainline ones."

Around the end of the nineteenth century "there was a fairly weak national church. By 1920 the church had a generation of strong leaders and this continued through the 1960s." The same is true, he is convinced, in other areas of society.

"You can't condemn the church and say, 'We have lousy leaders.' We're not producing Eugene Carson Blakes any more, in the same sense that we're not producing Thomas Jeffersons any more.

"I'm a believer in cyclical history. What we're going through now—by the time I'm 60 it may change."

He sees the Presbyterian emphasis on educated clergy remaining. "It's been a part of our tradition a long, long time to have an educated ministry. I expect it will continue. But, how it will continue we don't know."

And social witness? "We're going to see a downturn in so-called conservatism in this country. We're already beginning to see it. I think the American people are going to become outraged enough to move to left of center, and the same thing will happen in the church."

Who then has the most effect on the world, the church or the society?

"I liken it to two bodies of water that come together. Each is affected by the force of the other.

"I like to think the church has an impact; not in enormous ways, but progress is measured in bits and pieces.

"I'm always telling my kids, 'It's not really important how much money you make in life. I think God's not going to ask me that, but 'What did you do to help?'

"I think helping the church remember its past can make a difference."

The Collingswood Presbyterian Church has 323 members. Its pastor is the Reverend George H. Kuykendall.

Hearn Chun 🍂

Hearn Chun, third generation Christian, was born in Seoul, Korea. His grandfather, who once had been a follower of Confucius, became a Christian in his early teens. "I think the educational opportunities influenced him," the grandson says. "Presbyterian missionaries had established schools, and the school he entered was run by a Korean who had been converted. Chang Ho Ahn, the founder of the school, was a national leader who fought against Japanese colonization, came to the States and got an education, then returned to Korea and established Dae Sung." It was one of the more famous schools established by early Korean Christians. Hearn adds starkly, "It is not in existence now; it was in North Korea."

Both Hearn's parents were born into Christian families, and he grew up in the church. After earning a bachelor of arts degree at Seoul National University, he, like his grandfather, migrated to the United States for further education. He got a bachelor of divinity degree at Perkins (United Methodist)

School of Theology in Dallas, then went to Princeton Theological Seminary for a master of theology degree.

He had come to this country with his fiance, Jungsook, who also studied at Perkins. They were married in 1967 and had their first child in 1971 while Hearn was moving to Princeton. They have two daughters now: In August 1992, Ellen began her senior year at Smith College, and Eunjee began her senior year at Glenbrook North Senior High School.

All along it had been his plan to return to Korea after his graduate studies.

But . . . "I decided I needed to get a job and take care of my family" and so he left seminary before getting his doctorate, moved to Chicago, and with his brother's help started a business.

"I had made only a tentative decision not to go back home. But once I started the business, it snowballed and I couldn't get out of it."

Initially he combined his firm with his brother's import business but soon he established his own export business, selling construction equipment and supplies to "a lot of Korean contractors who were working in the Middle East at that time."

He continued in his business until 1989 when McCormick Theological Seminary asked him to take up another challenge: to become associate director of the seminary's Korean-American Ministries Center, helping prepare students for work in Korean-American churches and communities. That's his work now, along with being assistant professor of ministry at the school.

Meantime the Chuns have become U.S. citizens and members, since 1972, of the Hanmee Presbyterian Church in the Chicago suburb of Itasca. He is on the session and has finished a one-year term of service as clerk of the session.

"This church," he explains," is one of the few Korean congregations that follows the rotation system (allowing a maximum of three consecutive years as a session member) rather well." And with a grin he describes a situation true of many Presbyterian churches, "but those who rotate off always come back on later."

The church was established by a group of Korean immigrants in 1964, originally as an independent congregation with Presbyterian tendencies, and later becoming a part of the United Presbyterian Church U.S.A. When it was established, it was only the second Korean congregation in all of Chicago, the other being Methodist. Now there are eleven Korean Presbyterian congregations in Chicago Presbytery, with something like twenty-two hundred members.

One of the major concerns of Hearn Chun's church life is Hanmi Presbytery, the non-geographical administrative body (although all its member congregations are on the West Coast) made up entirely of Korean congregations. Hanmi was created about a decade ago, to help Korean Presbyterians make the transition from the language and customs of Korea as they become members of the PC(USA). Initially Hanmi was established for a ten-year lifespan, after which its congregations were to be phased into existing geographical presbyteries. However, Hanmi requested and received a fifteen-year extension from the 1992 General Assembly.

"We have somewhat divided opinions," Hearn says. "I am one of a very small minority of dissidents and I should let you know that others have other opinions."

He thinks the entire Hanmi movement is largely supported by its pastors; Korean congregations, he explains, are "pretty much the kind who leave all the matters up to the pastors to decide, and I think in most cases congregations don't concern themselves" with ecclesiastical activities. "Pastors have their congregations because on Sundays people come to this Korean-speaking congregation where they can do things together. Naturally, the tendency of pastors is to make sure they perpetuate this."

Hanmi came into being, he believes, "as a way around the system. They would say that if the denomination would allow them to have a separate presbytery that could be conducted in the Korean language and could be run by a Korean executive, then we could bring a lot more Korean congregations into the denomination. I think Hanmi Presbytery was created, not to replace the existing system, but as an additional way of increasing membership."

Efforts toward the fifteen-year extension began taking shape about three years before it was voted, he adds. "Anticipating that this issue would come up in the Milwaukee General Assembly, they (the Hanmi advocates) initiated a campaign, sort of through the National Korean Presbyterian Caucus, to get the support of all the Korean congregations" for extending the life of the presbytery. "Korean pastors who were already PC(USA) members were persuaded that this language presbytery has many advantages: You can run it under your own operating style, and decide many important matters such as ordination and property. Those points were very attractive. They decided, 'if we can have this sort of thing, why should we belong to an existing presbytery where we would be very uncomfortable.' So I think the campaign has gained momentum and has started collecting support almost on a nationwide basis.

"Suppose churches in Chicago, New York, Washington, D.C. could not join Hanmi Presbytery because of distance. So they started a movement where they would organize their own presbytery, let's say, in the New York area. Now this is a different kind of movement.

"Those churches and pastors who have membership in the PC(USA) would leave their presbyteries and organize new presbyteries and join them. So all of a sudden it's not only a movement to accommodate congregations and pastors who are not otherwise acceptable to the denomination, but at the same time it became a separatist movement: 'We want to have our own ethnic thing.'

"I am not sympathetic to that. The problem is that it will only reinforce Korean immigrant church life as a way of isolating people rather than helping them integrate into the society at large.

"The need for learning the (English) language is very urgent, but that's not the kind of need that's being looked at; we push it aside."

One of the main problems of the separatist trend, Hearn Chun believes, is that it hurts families. "Our young people, many of them born here, get their formative education here in the States. When the church is being the encourager of ethnicity, it is not promoting any kind of intergenerational dialogue. So we try to leave our younger generations' problems in the hands of their peer leaders. 'How am I going to be a member of this larger society?' is a basic question of that generation."

But he is convinced the younger generation cannot do that by themselves.

"They need grown-up role models. The church on the whole does not encourage younger generations to see that they don't have to limit their role models to their own race. Hanmi reinforces this kind of thing. The church should say to kids, 'you can be like any leaders—you don't have to limit your models just in terms of skin.'

Although the Hanmi experience dates farther back than the demise of the USSR and the resulting divisions of nations, he sees the ethnic separation movement in the church as being fueled by the breakups of nations in Eastern Europe, and is distressed by what it could mean.

"Ethnicity has good and bad sides. Hyphenated names, as in Korean-American Presbyterian, help us remember our heritage. But the downside is that it gives people illusions that they can live comfortably in ethnic enclaves. That is very destructive, because it rips apart the social fabric we need to stay together as a society, as a community.

"We've got to start our church life together at the presbytery level. I hope some day we can live together at a congregational level. We need to bring resources, wisdom, and insights together and to tackle the problems together."

Hanmee Presbyterian Church has 468 members. Its pastor is the Reverend Shinwon Kang.

❦ John Coy Cook

The question is asked like this: You've been described as "the only Navajo who is a Presbyterian minister." Does that mean in Grand Canyon Presbytery, or the Synod of the Southwest, or Arizona, or . . . ?

J. Coy Cook answers quickly and with a grin: "It basically means in the world. Actually, only the third ordained Navajo Presbyterian minister ever. The other two who were ordained are gone."

Coy Cook adds that his tribal name is Coy and that at one time Coy was the only name he had. His family was "very traditional regarding language, style of living in the Navajo culture." He was born near Piñon, Arizona, on the Navajo Reservation that sprawls across 17.5 million acres of Arizona and New Mexico where his family "raised sheep, cattle, did a little farming." He went first to a boarding school in Piñon, and studied later in Shiprock, New Mexico, then back in Arizona, where he was graduated from Holbrook High School.

"I worked in a sawmill a couple of years, then as an inter-preter for the church for one year," before he went back to formal education that included Phoenix Community College, Arizona State University, and Charles Cook School in Tempe where he did theological studies.

At Piñon, "I was enrolled in school as a Catholic. I went through the full catechism, was baptized as a Catholic, and took communion. I probably had decided around the tenth grade to go into the priesthood. Then I met my wife-to-be."

He "sort of spiritually floated for a couple of years. My wife's family had been Presbyterians a long time, so that's how I got to be a Presbyterian; sort of married into it, actually."

In April 1991, J.Coy Cook was named stated supply* pastor of the First Presbyterian Church of Tuba City, Arizona.

The Cooks have five children. In Tuba City Mrs. Cook "does a lot of visiting (in the parish) and keeps the family intact." In October 1991 she began working in a full-time job with the local reclamation office.

"In my reading of the Bible," says Coy Cook, "in trying to look at the important events in the movement of God, it seems to me that Moses and maybe Paul were involved in a very bicultural world. I think the intent of God is to have a multicultural world."

It is such a world that he works in, in the Tuba City congregation. The church, although deep in Navajo country, is by no means populated by Navajos only. U.S. Highway 160 running through the community separates Navajo lands from a small Hopi enclave. "We do have a number of Hopi families that come to church. There are a number of black families, also whites married to blacks, one Hispanic family, mixed Hopi and Navajo families, also single anglos and Navajos."

A Public Health Service hospital for Native Americans is situated in Tuba City; it and the schools in the community are the bases for most of the church's constituents. "We try to work with the hospital in terms of seeing patients; we have a small facility we use for people to stay overnight.

Sometimes we find people discharged from the hospital with no way to get home; if we have gasoline in a vehicle, we take them home. That's the ministry."

When such things aren't occupying the time of the pastor, he is involved in getting the church buildings—the original part of the plant was constructed in 1913—in operating order, doing a large part of the electrical work himself. In addition, "We just replanted the front yard and are working on the parking area; there's much physical work to be done."

Before he began work there, the Tuba City church had been virtually inactive. "We started with four or five people," he reports. "The largest attendance we've had thus far (in October 1991) was forty-eight adults and fourteen children. For the most part we've been able to keep those who have worshiped with us."

Worship is a blend of the cultures in which Coy Cook and the congregation he serves live:

"The order of worship is more anglo, but the prayers and sermons are bicultural. It's new to all the people, and they find it much more interesting that way. I use a lot of ecojustice issues; they are important to our church. Native people are beginning to see that they can contribute something, that ecojustice is connected to their faith.

"The need is here. Operating as the church really needs to be is in a bicultural pattern. There are ways to do it, but it's not going to be the same as an ordinary Presbyterian expects.

"I think the work we're doing is needed. We've already seen results. I have to do it through my own tradition. I don't find anybody objecting to it. I feel satisfied with the work here. I think if I'm allowed to be myself I can contribute to my culture, contribute to the community and the Presbyterian church."

* Supplier of pastoral services for a specified period of time.

The First Presbyterian Church of Tuba City, Arizona, now has 13 members on its rolls.

Jay Kintzel ❦

What moves people to enter the ministry? There may be as many answers as there are ministers, but for Jay Kintzel it was, "Quite simply, the influence of the Holy Spirit."

Born in Cedar Rapids, Iowa, Jay grew up in Stanwood, about thirty miles east of his birthplace, the youngest of five children. "It was a small farming community," he remembers, "largely German Protestants. Both Vickie (his wife) and I are of German parentage.

"My parents grew up in the Evangelical Church, which merged with the Evangelical Reformed; by the time I was growing up that church merged with the Congregationalists to form the United Church of Christ."

After high school he entered the University of Iowa, met and married Vickie, and enlisted in the Army before graduating. Their two children, Jason and Anjy, were born in Germany while Jay was stationed there.

"Eventually we came back to a Cedar Rapids suburb and joined the Kenwood Park Presbyterian Church in 1978. We were active in a young couples' group and one thing led to another. Vickie was asked to be a deacon; later I was asked to be an elder; after that Vickie was elected an elder. We both got to be quite active.

"Vickie recognized her call to the ministry in 1983–84 and we began looking at seminaries. We visited McCormick (in Chicago), UTS (Union Theological Seminary) in Richmond, Virginia, and Louisville Seminary. She really liked McCormick but because of the children we were concerned about the urban environment. She came to San Francisco and liked it, and also liked having the opportunity to study in the Graduate Theological Union."

Jay intended to continue his work with computers and systems analysis while she was in school. "I felt it was my responsibility to be the provider for the family."

They planned their move to San Anselmo with the understanding that his company would transfer him. "But the bottom dropped out of the market. Still, we were committed to making the transition and decided to go ahead with it."

While Vickie began her seminary studies, Jay worked in some other jobs in San Francisco—"while doing some struggling with what I was supposed to be doing with my life. Eventually, a series of events really came together that led me to acknowledge my call."

For him, the sense of call was in the form of "a growing dissatisfaction" with any other kind of work. "Through the church work I'd been involved in, I derived satisfaction from working with people, helping people to realize their best qualities. I guess the really deciding factor was that I couldn't be happy in what I was doing."

Although he had not completed his undergraduate college studies, he was able to finish his degree requirements via an extended program and a graduate record exam. And "the SFTS admissions committee decided to admit me."

"Beginning seminary, it all felt right. There was no doubt in my mind that it was what I was supposed to be about."

As part of his seminary training, Jay Kintzel arranged to spend a year as an intern on the staff of the Presbytery of

San Francisco, with responsibilities that included steward-ship. After that he would go back for his final year of study before being eligible for a master of divinity degree.

Does he think he'll be headed for the pastorate, once his seminary work is behind him?

"Of some nature, yes. But I don't necessarily think what I'm called to is the traditional pastorate; I think it'll be a specialized ministry of some nature.

"I'm finding work at the presbytery level to be very en-joyable. Also, there's some possibility of overseas ministry."

Does that mean missionary work? "Yes and no. Concilia-tory work, maybe. Helping bring people of different cul-tures together . . . one of the most important things I see is that I can be a part of helping people realize they are chil-dren of God—what that can mean for them in their relation-ships with other people.

Moving from Cedar Rapids to San Francisco led him to see "a tremendous difference in cultures." The church "really needs to play a role in using the richness of that (cultural) di-versity, that can be enriching for the whole community."

The individual church, he is convinced, "needs to be more aware of the community it's a part of. It needs to change; to change the way it goes about ministry, but even more basic, the way it sees and identifies itself.

A unique thing about the church, says Jay Kintzel, is "the opportunity to reflect the love of God that is there, is pre-sent around us, which is for us.

"When I was younger, I couldn't understand what inter-est God could have in me. Now I do. God sees value in us and has given each of us special gifts; through God's gifts we are unique human beings and we each can be active par-ticipants in life as God intends it."

❧ *Jim Finney*

Some people say the church should not be involved in the affairs of the world. Not so Jim Finney.

In fact, participation in the rest of life is an important part of what a church should do, says the tall, sandy-haired, real estate appraiser from Santa Fe, New Mexico. Of his church membership he says, "I've always had the thought that the services and environment here suited me; involvement in local and national affairs is compatible with my feelings."

"Our church has always served as a forum for important issues. They don't try to push opinions or ideas, but are open to discussion. I always appreciate that."

He doesn't keep up with activities at the national level of the Presbyterian Church (U.S.A.) in great detail. But "I've read and heard discussions about some of the issues of the past year. We've had a lot of discussions regarding Central America (the refugees coming to this country and the Sanctuary movement), and also sexuality (the highly publicized report and action on human sexuality before and during the church's 1991 General Assembly). Those types of things don't disturb me at all. They're a sign of keeping up on things we've been faced with. It's good to deal with them."

James H. Finney became a Presbyterian when he and Mary, his wife, joined the First Presbyterian Church of Santa Fe in 1962. She had been a Methodist, and he "a very occasional Congregationalist."

"Mary and I selected the Presbyterian church as sort of a compromise between the Methodists and—others. We came here, loved the worship services. Bob Boshen was the pastor then, and called on us. The church kind of filled out the pattern of what we were looking for.

"Mary has always been a strong church member. Oklahoma, where I grew up, was very heavily Methodist and Baptist; I always felt sort of rebellious toward them."

Mary and Jim have two children, Britten, who works in Santa Fe and Gardner, who is married and in the U.S. Navy. Jim's description of the younger Finneys' involvement in church would fit those of a great many Presbyterian parents: "Both are members here, but do not come."

In a time when many congregations are losing members, he believes Santa Fe First is steady. "We've been with the church thirty years. Membership was so low at one point that it needed a shot in the arm. It picked up around the second third of the time we've been here, and now it's pretty well holding its own."

He analyzes the membership losses of churches in general straightforwardly: "There's so much movement toward other religions, people looking for some strong body to tell them what to do, to give them some kind of comfort and security."

And that brings him back to his own perception of what a church should be, and what the major jobs of a church are.

"It should be a place of Sunday morning worship, a nice place where a person can worship once a week; the atmosphere for that is important.

"Second, it should be a forum for issues—world, national, local—a place for people to discuss, and learn.

"Third, it should be a catalyst for giving help to people. The Hunger Fund is one of the best things they do."

What of the future of the church? He is quiet for a time, thinking.

"I can only see pretty much a continuation of what I've known. The struggle, it seems to me, will be to keep up with changing times, with more integration of cultures and races.

"I think we've made great strides toward eliminating bigotry and such, even though it's painful to go through. The women's movement, racial attitudes, we've made great advances. In the homosexual issue, we've learned much about that. The church seems to be right in the middle of it all.

"I guess what I'm really saying is that the church serves as an educational arm, and that I really appreciate that."

The First Presbyterian Church of Santa Fe has 1,023 members. Its interim pastor is the Reverend George Gilmour.

Joan Steele 🍂

They met at a church camp at Wasatch Academy in Mount Pleasant, Utah. She was in the tenth grade; he was a year older than she. They were married when she graduated from Westminster College in Salt Lake City, after he had finished a year's study at Princeton Theological Seminary.

Did their romance blossom there at junior high camp?

"Yes," says Joan Steele. "And it still does."

Their life together has taken Joan and David Steele from the eastern United States to the West—from New Jersey to California, in fact, with stops in Maryland, Utah, and Hawaii. Joan has taught in public and private schools, studied at San Francisco State College for a paralegal certificate, and now works in the Marin County (California) court system. This while her husband has been a pastor of a rural church, founding pastor of a new church, chaplain in Hawaii, and now pastor of the Christ in Terra Linda Presbyterian Church in San Rafael, California.

They have two sons now—Mark, an engineer in southern

California, and Andrew, a teacher in New York's Harlem area—and three grandchildren. (Like his father, Andrew also is a writer by avocation).

Joan Patton was born in southern Idaho, "in Mormon country, in a non-Mormon family." Her parents eventually separated and she lived for a time with her mother and grandparents. Later, when her mother remarried, they moved to Salt Lake City; she lived there through her college years.

She and David returned to Salt Lake City when he was asked to start what became the Cottonwood Presbyterian Church there.

Was being Presbyterians in a heavily Mormon area tough duty? "Yes," she says, and quickly adds, "It was pretty exciting, too. People are in church (in such situations) because they want to be; they express their faith because they are called upon to do it."

The Steeles were there six years, until David accepted a call to be chaplain of the Punahou School in Hawaii. In Hawaii Joan taught at Iolani, an Episcopal school for boys. They lived there twelve years before moving to San Rafael.

She thought of continuing to teach in San Rafael, "but at that time the county was closing schools." So she went to San Francisco State for paralegal studies and started her new career.

"I work where we receive court filings, with the superior court and back up in the probate court. It's all civil law."

Does she like it? "Yeah," with a smile. But, "It's hard work. Lots of working with people who are upset, people who think we're attorneys and can help them, people who get frustrated when we can't help them."

How does she feel about being a pastor's wife?

"I consider myself a member of the church, the same as any other member. I suppose there are more things David would like me to do, and that's changed as our marriage has changed, as we've matured."

Is being a pastor's wife something like living in a fishbowl?

"I guess we haven't had that kind of experience. People have been supportive of us.

"I've had a rich life. It's been a privilege."

Of her Presbyterian background, she says, "When David and I met, I was a Methodist. I joined the Presbyterian church after we got married."

Her membership is deeply rooted by now: "I guess it's what being Presbyterian is; I believe in the mainline church; it finds the path that I believe in. I believe in the theory of finding God's truth through the group process."

As with the denomination as a whole, she notes that San Rafael is "a graying community." And partly for that reason, "Numerically, the future looks iffy, doesn't it?"

But she sees hope in the church's future, with change as one of the reasons. In San Rafael, "the church finally decided to take a stand as a More Light* congregation. And we see so many women going into the ministry now; it's interesting, projecting what that will mean.

"The church is adapting itself more, in evolution. It's more open to change than the country is."

* More Light congregations are those specifically welcoming homosexual people into their membership.

The Christ in Terra Linda Presbyterian Church, of which the Reverend David Steele is pastor, has 212 members.

❦ John Fife

In an era when deploring the plight of churches is commonplace, John Fife believes his denomination is right where it needs to be.

"From my vantage point, the Presbyterian church is in a better position than any other to be in ministry for the next decade or so," he says. "Like all denominations we've had a difficult time in the past fifteen years or so. But the Presbyterian church has moved out ahead in ways that will help us."

John Fife of Tucson, Arizona, is tall and lean, with a neat grey beard and an easy informality. His omnipresent cowboy boots contributed to *Newsweek* magazine's dubbing him "the Marlboro Minister" half a dozen years ago; he is much deeper than the stereotype.

In 1992 he was elected moderator of the General Assembly, the highest elective post in the denomination. He had been in the national spotlight before, in a markedly different way. In the mid-1980s he was in the forefront of a movement giving sanctuary to refugees from war-ravaged Central American countries. Charged with breaking immigration laws and tried in federal court along with a number of others, he was found guilty, sentenced to five years in prison, and placed on probation.

He briefly addressed the church's General Assembly in 1986 about his work on behalf of the refugees and its possible cost to him. In the 1992 Assembly he spoke of the sanctuary experience again, but against a different background. Praising the denomination's support of the sanctuary concept, he said, "Our work has been vindicated, and our first amendment rights upheld. And the church has made a difference."

How the church can make a difference in other fields, years to come, is on his mind regularly.

"We decentralized early on (1973), and shifted the use of finances to the local level. We went through reunion and re-organization and I think, by and large, we've got the pull and tug of that pretty well accomplished. We're ready now to look outward again.

"And we're extraordinarily well equipped to deal with this brand new world.

"A world without borders is what the economic and political groups are looking at. The Presbyterian church has done all the hard work of building relationships with other Christians around the world, and understands itself as a global church, ready to deal with a new world; to be a force in spirit and ethics in the new global community that is emerging."

Through all the internal changes, he finds his denomination has kept the faith in its outward responsibilities.

"In relation to the culture, we've maintained our integrity. We really did continue to say we cared about such things as justice, and peacemaking, in the midst of all the cultural excesses—when the culture was trying to develop some amnesia about those concerns."

On another front, he is convinced the denomination in which he serves has made remarkable progress in dealing with controversy.

"This year (1992) we showed an incredible ability to deal

with deep divisions, and to heal, even as we agree that there is no consensus. We've really become very skilled in handling trouble, and in managing conflict.

"I'm delighted with where the Presbyterian church is positioned now, for over the next decade. We never lost our ecumenical and global commitment through that whole period."

And, he is convinced, the church will need to be busy.

"It's clear that within the U.S. we're going to go, in the next ten years, through a period of great pain. In the past decade we mortgaged our future in this nation, and abandoned our basic institutions that make up the health and strength of a society: education, health care, and infrastructure.

"To rebuild is going to take major sacrifices in all segments. It will take spiritual leadership—and the church is uniquely called to ask people to make sacrifices, and to do so in such a way that no one is exploited and the pain is distributed; to provide for the basic general welfare of the nation.

"Globally, where capital flows freely around the world, people begin to realize how closely we really are bound together—which the church has always understood. How we develop morally and ethically in that world commitment is the business of the church.

"It's not something new for us. We're not a church just now starting to send out missionaries; we have relationships with that whole global community."

None of this is to say that John Fife thinks the church has solved all its problems or that it has no untended needs.

"There's a piece in which I hope to make some contribution: providing spiritual leadership to the church. I hope I can help provide that sense of unity and spiritual direction that our church needs, that I think it is genuinely searching for. I think there's a sense out there that we're ready to put it all together now." And after a moment's pause, " but that always happens spiritually, not institutionally."

His concern for, and involvement in, things spiritual may seem at first glance to be out of keeping for one so energetically active. Instead, his activity in the sanctuary movement spurred a deeper interest in things of the spirit.

At the time he was awaiting trial, he said, "I don't want to sound too pious about this, because piety is not endemic to my personality. But in the suffering, death, and tragedy I've seen in the last four years, I've been converted to a new spirituality, a brand-new awareness of the presence of Christ and the Spirit of God moving in Central America, and in the life of my congregation."

If he speaks of such now, he is only preaching what he practices: "I've spent some considerable time developing that mystical dimension to my faith experience." He spends some time each week at a Roman Catholic retreat center in the desert outside Tucson and, reminded that most of the great religions trace their origins to the desert, he quickly replies, "The desert has become very important to me."

Fife's love of the desert country began during a summer job with the church's Board of National Missions on the Dohono O'dam (formerly called Papago) Indian reservation in Arizona. This was after his first year in Pittsburgh Theological Seminary, and "confirmed some things that had been stirring around in my soul." The stirrings had started earlier, during some conversations with a pastor friend when "I discovered to my astonishment that Christianity made a lot of sense, and at some point about then I made a serious commitment to try and be a disciple of Jesus."

Following seminary he worked in an inner-city project in Ohio, but Arizona was where he really wanted to be. Southside had begun as a Native American mission and had evolved to include Hispanics, Blacks, and Whites—56 members in all, and for both congregation and future pastor their meeting was something like love at first sight. He has been there since 1970.

Neither the limelight of the sanctuary movement nor that of being moderator has made any change in John Fife's main priorities. As he was then, he is the husband of Marianne Fife; the father of their two sons—John III and David—and a pastor in a less-than-affluent section of Tucson. He talks with excitement of the building project under way at Southside—"it's a reconstruction of an Anasazi kiva;

we're replicating it for our new worship center"—and of his work there.

So his answer is no surprise when he is asked what he wants to do once his year in the moderatorial spotlight is finished:

"Marianne and I in the last couple of years have spent a lot of time talking about how to finish out my ministry. What I want to do is the same thing as I said I wanted to do after the sanctuary action was over. I just want to be the pastor of Southside Presbyterian Church."

Louise Josephson ❦

"I strongly believe my first call is being a never-married woman at Princeton Theological Seminary."

Louise Josephson, in her mid-forties in the spring of 1992 and nearing the end of her senior year, is talking about her seminary days and her hopes for the future. She is moderator (president) of the senior class.

Single students are required to live in a dormitory at Princeton Seminary, she explains, "so I live on a floor with twenty-eight other women. In such close quarters you get to know them pretty well." She firmly believes that her presence among considerably younger classmates is a call, and that her age has been an asset in that regard.

She regards her age as a liability, however, in seeking "a second call." She is hoping that call will be to be in a parish: "As an experienced layperson with eighteen years of administrative background, I'm looking for a pastorate."

In addition to seeing the pastorate as a place in need of administrative skills, she views it as a teaching situation "and my love is teaching. I have a gift for teaching. I also have a real concern for adult Christian education and I think we overlook that in our churches."

She grew up around arts, "having a mother who worked with her hands" and majored in crafts and interior design at the University of Tennessee. "I went into interior design, switched to crafts and there received my bachelor's degree. I wanted to teach, so I also got a master's in crafts."

While she was in graduate school, Louise Josephson was offered a job as director of the crafts center at the University Center. She stayed in the job for eighteen years.

She joined the Second Presbyterian Church in Knoxville with her family while she was a child. Her mother had been a Methodist, her father a Lutheran. "Our family lived in South Africa while I was very young and I went to school at a convent. When we moved to Knoxville my parents wanted a church where the children would be happy; we joined Second Presbyterian. I was always active in the church and the community, and used my art in church." She also was elected and ordained a deacon, and an elder.

Eventually she reached the point "where I found my job was getting in the way of church and what I wanted to be doing. I thought about going to seminary after I retired.

"My involvement in the church continued to grow, especially in the five years prior to my coming here (to Princeton)."

She discussed this with her pastor. "He said, 'Maybe God is tired of hearing you talk about seminary when you retire and is giving you an opportunity to work in the church now.'"

Her administrative experience will be especially helpful in the pastorate, she believes, in several ways. Among them: "A pastor has to know how to deal with thorny issues. I'm a very direct person, and tend to address things head on. I would want to get my facts totally straight before opening my mouth. There are some issues a congregation won't even know about and you have to treat such things delicately, carefully. In all this you have to be a loving, caring person who knows your congregation.

"(But) the first thing to keep in mind is the proclamation

of the Word. By taking the Word into the community and making it a part of life."

So what does the Presbyterian Church (U.S.A.) look like to the moderator of a seminary senior class about to go in search of a pastorate?

"The church is people of faith who are really struggling with their relationship to Jesus Christ, who are trying to discern what that means in their own lives and also what that means for their lives in the world. People who like to get together as people, to be supported. It's not always just 'what can we do with this world?' We go to church because we enjoy each other's company; we like to laugh. It's not all serious.

"I like to think that being a member of the church is the most exciting thing that we can be, and that we want to share that with each other—with those people within, and those not within.

"I really love the polity of the Presbyterian church. I like the lay representation on all levels."

She speaks of being a seminary intern at the 1991 General Assembly and has two clear recollections from that experience:

"The most stimulating things I brought back from the General Assembly were that I was able to see that we work more from the bottom up than from the top down. In any organization you need people who are doing the research and bringing the information together, but people from all over, gathered to express their concern. All were given equal opportunity to speak, within limits of course, and they really had persuasive power.

"The other thing I remember was that there were very well versed young people representing our church at the General Assembly. The commissioners listened, and really wanted to know the concerns of today's young people. That was exciting."

Since being interviewed, Louise Josephson has accepted the position of Coordinator of Christian Education at The Brick Presbyterian Church in New York City.

❦ Mark Vernon

When Mark Vernon was being considered for his first pastorate, a member of the pastor search committee for the First Presbyterian Church of Dalhart, Texas, asked him what he thought of having an American flag and a Christian or Presbyterian flag in the sanctuary.

The minister replied that he wouldn't accept a call to a church with such adornments in its worship area.

Soon thereafter the Dalhart congregation voted to call him as their pastor. "I believe in America," he is quick to add, "but the flag in the sanctuary becomes an idol." There is a flag in the church's fellowship hall "and that's OK. The fellowship hall isn't a worship place."

Mark Vernon has strong convictions about the faith and the church, and works hard to uphold them.

There have been other occasions when convictions and customs collided in Dalhart, and he hopes and believes growth has resulted.

At one point he learned that the congregation—like some

others do—was paying its mission apportionment at the end of the year, if any money was left. He told a member of the session that he felt serious enough about the issue to decline his monthly salary check unless the monthly apportionment had been paid. The elder brought the issue up at a subsequent session meeting and arrangements were made to make the payments differently. "I'm of the conviction that this will be a standard condition in future calls."

He is expressing his faith by being a pastor after what he calls two years of "kicking and screaming" resistance. He had been in and out of church life before a sense of call to the ministry began to tug at him.

Mark was born in Atlanta, Georgia, the son of an airline pilot. The family later moved to Texas, where he was "raised in the church." His parents were Methodists. "Then my sister got polio. She was in Fort Worth in Children's Hospital. The Methodist minister never came to visit. The Presbyterian minister did. By the time she got out of the hospital, we were Presbyterians."

He was attending a Presbyterian church in Arlington, Texas, "when an associate pastor started a rift in the church. I was in my early twenties, and became very disillusioned with the church structure. That was probably my faith crisis. I walked away from the church and didn't attend for about ten years. I didn't like the way it was organized, didn't like being Presbyterian, although I was Presbyterian to my bones."

Sheryl, his wife, "had been a pretty avid churchgoer" before their marriage in 1978. He still was not. "But God's got a wonderful sense of humor. I woke up one morning and said, 'We're going to church.' She agreed. I walked into the church and felt like I was home again."

After about two more years "I started feeling a sense of call to the ministry, which I fought, denied. I had gone into sales management, was making good money, felt it was not a time to change careers. But the sense kept getting stronger."

He discussed his dilemma with the Reverend Warren

Neal, who had been his pastor earlier in life. Although the two had never spoken of Mark's going into the ministry before, "he said 'I've been watching you wrestle with that for a couple of years.'" After that, Mark went to a career testing center operated by Grace Presbytery. The results showed he was best suited for the ministry.

"I had no college degree at the time, so I thought I'd go back to school and try it. And made straight A's." So seminary became inevitable. After completing his undergraduate work in two years, he entered and later was graduated from Austin Presbyterian Seminary in Austin, Texas. Meanwhile he was gaining valuable experience: "I did pulpit supplies, liked preaching, and preached most every Sunday."

Dalhart is a community of about 6,200 in the northwest corner of Texas. The First Presbyterian Church has about 100 members. Eighteen families have joined during his time there, Mark reports.

His first pastorate "has been a little bumpy at times, but I think they all are." He found out quickly that his sales background was no help in his new career—"from selling bulldozers to preaching the Word is quite a jump"—although his administrative skills were useful. His style is straightforward:

"I don't make any bones about it, I do a high profile visitation," he says. "I try to get around to see every family in the church; here, you can do that about three times a year."

At the time of this conversation he had been in Dalhart approximately two years. "I've got about one more year here before it's time for me to go," he believes. "I've really shaken the trees, and they (the congregation) needed that. When I came here, I knew it was not going to be long-term. I've taken them from being a Baptist congregation to being pretty much Presbyterian.

"I have very strong feelings about the church," he says, and has relied on the Presbyterian constitution steadily. When he first went to Dalhart "the church did not have a sense of being a part of a connected denomination," he recalls. He remembers saying, in a session meeting early in his ministry there, 'Wait a minute, what's the *Book of Order* say?' The response was, 'We don't use that here very much.' And I said, 'We're going to now.'

"It's been a roller coaster ride. There have been some wonderful moments. We've had a 40 percent increase overall in active attendance; we have 60 percent of our adults attending Sunday school now, and they're enjoying it. We've made some good headway. But I've pushed them about all I can.

"The victory side here is that the people are beginning to understand what it means to be Presbyterian. We now have active Christian education and evangelism committees; this summer we had a vacation Bible school with sixty kids, thirty of them our own and thirty not."

He is less hopeful about the future of small congregations than about that of the denomination as a whole.

"We're going to suffer some in rural churches," he believes, "but nationally, the outlook is very bright and positive." He sees the Presbyterian church as a viable way to bring non-Christians to Christ, "because we always have and will address the issues—as long as we make the Word become flesh now, and not in 1930 terms.

"Young people are looking for a place where they can have a voice, where they can get an understanding of the grace of God. People out here are heavily influenced by the doctrine of punishment, of the wrath of God. For years we've proclaimed our polity; it's time to start proclaiming our theology. What we do the lousiest job in proclaiming is our strongest suit: an understanding of the grace of God."

In Dalhart as in any place, he believes, "As long as the people are asking questions, I figure they're exploring their faith."

And all that, he says, is why he is in the ministry after resisting it so vigorously. "It got to the point that there was nothing in the world I wanted to do more. There is nothing more fulfilling. I know I'm doing what God put me on earth to do."

❦ *Melva Costen*

Melva Costen, fourth generation Presbyterian, remembers an unwritten rule from her childhood: "Growing up in the Presbyterian church meant that almost every child had to learn to do something which would edify the congregation and the community. Whatever gifts you had were to be shared with others. Growing in the faith was commensurate with building up the body of Christ."

Her gift was music. She started piano lessons at age 12 and at 13 she was playing the piano for worship in Due West, South Carolina. She has been sharing her gift of music ever since.

"My folk were influenced and affected by the fact that Presbyterians provided African Americans in the South with education," she says. "Education was important to the family. Generations on both sides of the family were college-trained people from Presbyterian-related Johnson C. Smith University. They were invariably leaders of the community, and teachers."

Dimensions of the national church and of ecumenicity that were present in Melva's childhood and youth helped shape her feelings about being Presbyterian.

"My dad's being involved nationally was what I called 'divine serendipity'." Denominational officials were around frequently, so that it was not unusual for some member of the Board of National Missions to visit our home." The associations broadened her outlook, and her perspective of the national church.

Her father, John Theodore Wilson, was a Johnson C. Smith graduate, a chemistry teacher, coach, and finally a Sunday school missionary for the old (Northern) Presbyterian Board of National Missions. Her mother, Azzie Lee Ellis Wilson, was a graduate of Barber Scotia College and a public school teacher. Her grandparents' generation also was marked by college-trained members. So it was natural for Melva, even though she started her post-high school studies at Harbison (South Carolina) Junior College, to wind up at Johnson C. Smith—and to meet James H. Costen there.

"I grew up actively involved as a Presbyterian, but in southern black communities it was natural for people to share worship and mission with other denominations. We didn't call it ecumenism, but we were very much interactive with other denominations. So AME, (African Methodist Episcopal), Baptist, and Pentecostal churches were all home territory for us. But our Presbyterian preachers were always Johnson C. Smith Seminary graduates.

"We were always aware that as black Presbyterians we were born with a 'silver spoon' in our mouths, and that spoon was an educational spoon."

Melva Wilson and Jim Costen were married on their baccalaureate Sunday. She was already teaching elementary school and music in the Charlotte, North Carolina, area, where the university is located. After Jim completed his seminary education at Johnson C. Smith Theological Seminary (which also was in Charlotte at that time), they moved to Rocky Mount, North Carolina, his first parish, and she was almost immediately hired to teach there.

She continued teaching in public schools, with music classes always included either in the classrooms or in her studio at home. All this occurred as they were becoming the parents of two sons and a daughter.

In 1965, Jim accepted a call to develop a new church in Atlanta, Georgia. Melva continued her career as a music enrichment teacher in Atlanta public schools until 1973. That was the year when she was called to become assistant professor of music at Johnson C. Smith Theological Seminary, which had been moved to Atlanta to become part of the Interdenominational Theological Center (ITC). Her assignment was to teach courses in church music and African American religious music, and to develop a choir. Events were soon to add another dimension to her work.

"The teacher of worship at the seminary died unexpectedly, and I was asked to take over his classes. I agreed to do it if Jim could co-teach the class with me. By the end of the semester the students were so inspired, I guess by the excitement engendered in worship, that they wrote the seminary president and asked that this become a required course." It is a required subject now, and she still teaches it—along with two other courses in worship, courses in music and conducts seminary choir.

In 1984 a grant to ITC made possible the development of worship as a major area of study. This was a result of Melva's work as teacher of worship to students from six denominations at ITC: helping them grow in understanding worship in their own denominations, and also to share ecumenically with other denominations. The grant has made possible continuing consultations in African American worship traditions, and a chair in worship—the Helmar E. Nielsen Professor of Worship and Music—which Melva holds.

"Over a period of four years we were able to gather scholars —lay and clergy—from African American denominations plus African American Catholics, United Methodists, Lutherans, Episcopalians, and Presbyterians, to discuss two questions: 'What is black worship?' and 'What are the unique features that make us identify as one despite our denominational differences?' The fourth consultation, which was open to persons interested in or serving in a leadership role in their congregations or denominations, attracted one hundred twenty-five registrants. The total participation was more than three hundred, including a number of local church choirs, drama groups, and liturgical dancers."

As her teaching career progressed so did her denominational involvement. In 1977 her church choir and the ITC chorus were invited to sing at the United Presbyterian General Assembly in Philadelphia. Following her election to the church's Advisory Council on Discipleship and Worship, (which she later chaired), she was part of a task force on baptism, and another to write a new directory for worship. With post-reunion reorganization, she was elected to the new PC(USA) Theology and Worship Ministry Unit Committee, which she also subsequently chaired.

With her background, she was the obvious choice to head the denominational committee that put together the church's new, widely acclaimed *Presbyterian Hymnal,* published in 1990.

Melva believes there is "a real resurgence of interest" in the church, and "in worship that is reflective of the people. Also, among African American people there is a strong claiming of the Presbyterian heritage, a reclaiming of African and African American heritages, and efforts to demonstrate how all three heritages are compatible with Reformed worship."

But strong as her interest in worship is, music still is a major vehicle for sharing the gifts she was taught in childhood.

To how many people has she passed along her gift of music? She smiles and shrugs. "About twenty-five in that first congregation. I had a studio and taught maybe sixty-five students a week in Rocky Mount. In public schools I also taught music and touched another two or three thousand, I guess. This doesn't include all those congregations that have been touched through seminary graduates."

A more recent development ties together her multiple interests: "Zvi Shapiro, a Jewish rabbi on the faculty at ITC/

Johnson C. Smith Seminary, connected me with Kim Blitch, the director of the (Jewish) Sharim Chorale here in Atlanta. Her chorale has about seventy voices; there are forty in the ITC Chorus.

"In each of the past three years, prior to Passover we have had a joint concert. After singing alternately, we perform some compositions together—some in Hebrew and some in the poetic language of Black folks. We share our similar walks as people of God through struggles, and reflect on ways that African Americans have relied strongly on the Old Testament walk as a movement into the future with Christ.

"This year our concert was televised. I directed the joint choirs in 'Lift Every Voice and Sing' and Kim directed the choirs in singing the Jewish anthem in Hebrew.

"Our concluding song was 'The Star Spangled Banner' as a reminder that as an American nation our unity is made possible. Because of the American culture, we can make our various cultures come together as God's children."

Nancy Warlick 🍎

"My grandfather, Herman Guy Kump, was a ruling elder and a governor of West Virginia. He stood about 5 feet 6 inches, and he was quite a fighter for worthy causes . I guess my mother and I come by that trait honestly."

This is Nancy Warlick speaking. She is somewhere close to her grandfather's height, and certainly close to his trait of fighting for beliefs. She is interested in—and works hard for—a number of causes, but her crowning passion is freedom and democracy for the people of Zaire.

Along with William Warlick, her husband of more than thirty years, she went to what is now the Republic of Zaire as a Presbyterian missionary in 1965. They have lived and worked in the central African country off and on ever since, leaving it most recently in September 1991 when riots caused the withdrawal of missionaries.

They both did all they could toward the health, education, and spiritual nurture of the people among whom they lived. If anything, she has been even more zealous in her efforts on behalf of Zaire's people since they had to leave.

Some of her friends—and some officials she has encountered—call her "Badger" for her determined efforts.

Put simply, she wants Mobutu Sese Seko ousted from office as president of Zaire, in order that real democracy can be established in that nation.

But all that is getting ahead of the story.

Nancy Wooddell "at age 12 felt very clearly the Lord's call to go to the Belgian Congo" as a missionary. Her mother—who some years later would deliver a decisive speech to a Presbyterian General Assembly on behalf of boycotting Nestle products—was "a tremendous support" in this ambition. Nancy finished high school in Beverly, West Virginia, and went to Southwestern at Memphis (now Rhodes) College. "I majored in French, knowing that I wanted to go to the mission field, and that French was the language spoken in the Belgian Congo."

She met William Warlick at a global mission conference at the Presbyterian church's Montreat (North Carolina) Conference Center in 1960; they were married the next year. "He wanted to go to Brazil, but he thinks the deck was stacked because when we went before the board they asked Bill to go to Africa."

The Board of World Missions felt Bill needed local church experience before going overseas, so the couple moved to Anniston, Alabama, where he became an associate pastor at the First Presbyterian Church there under the tutelage of the Reverend Philip Noble. "Bill was called with the idea that he would do new church development in Anniston. He started meeting that summer with people interested in starting a new church." The Good Shepherd Presbyterian Church resulted, with Bill Warlick as its pastor until 1965 when he and Nancy were appointed missionaries.

They were sent first to Belgium to study French and the colonial government policies in the Belgian Congo. "Interestingly enough, President Mobutu came into power while we were in Brussels," says Nancy. "So I guess my journey began then, seeing Mobutu come in. I'd sure like to see him gone."

Would she want to be quoted on that?

"I certainly would. I've been pretty outspoken about the fact that he needs to leave the scene."

Looking back, she says, "I guess when he first came in, people were hopeful and thought he would bring stability, peace, a higher living standard. By 1969 I think I had realized he would not do what people hoped for and needed."

The Warlick family—parents and two children, Elizabeth and William—spent their first term "at a station among former cannibals, in Moma, a very remote area. This is where we—parents and children—learned to speak and understand Tshiluba. Let me say, too, that those three years were three of the happiest we've ever had."

They came back to the United States on their first furlough in the summer of 1969. "In the capital, Kinshasa, that year, some university students from the Kasai provinces demonstrated against Mobutu. He supposedly sent troops out to kill the students. About two hundred were killed. Mobutu denied doing it, but we knew about it because we knew people whose kids never returned home."

In 1970 they went to Mbujimayi ("Goat Water, in English")."I had taught Bible at the local junior high school at Moma, but in 1971 I had to teach my own children. There was a school in Moma for Zairian children. We wanted to put Elizabeth in it, but the local principal said it would be a bad idea and asked us not to send her."

Nancy had developed a malignancy in 1970, before they returned to Zaire. "Then by March 1971 I was pregnant and pretty sick, so they sent me home with the children. Bill stayed; he had been made field secretary in charge of all Presbyterian missionary personnel in Zaire. There were more than one hundred mission people there."

She regained her health and went back to Zaire, where their third child, Samuel Shamba, was born. "We named him for an African pastor with whom Bill worked." They lived for a year in Lubondai, and later a year in Kananga, where "I ended up being the principal, founder, whatever you call it, of the school for missionaries' children there. It fell to me to get a school started; I had help from a Mennonite missionary lady and a pilot's wife. We had seven students the first year."

Bill was a missionary in residence in Atlanta in 1972–73. "In 1974 we took a ten-year leave of absence and Bill started a new church development (now New Hope Presbyterian Church) in Chattanooga, Tennessee. In 1984 John Pritchard (at that time in charge of missionary work in Africa) of the Division of International Mission asked us to go back to coordinate a multifaceted project of evangelism and church growth.

"The project came about because a Presbyterian elder named Alex Booth from Huntington, West Virginia, gave a million dollars up front, and challenged the Division of International Mission and the Outreach Foundation to raise another million to match it. "It was set up as a five-year project, and later extended.

"Bill went on a forty-five-day fact-finding trip to see how church leaders in Africa felt we could assist them. The project expanded to Ghana as well as Zaire; it now is under way in eleven African countries.

"The work was to build churches, train pastors, and meet the needs of the expanding church in Africa. We got into school construction in October 1986; it was obvious that the schools in Zaire were in terrible shape. The government had nationalized church schools in 1970, then turned them back to the church. Buildings were in terrible repair, and few if any children had textbooks. In the project we also built about thirty church buildings in Kinshasha alone, and did the same kind of thing in the interior, plus conducted Bible schools and a pastors' institute.

"It's been an incredible experience for us to be involved in. When we first got to Kinshasha, we talked to some American Baptists who said, 'This sounds like a Baptist project!'

"It was obvious when we moved to Kinshasa in 1985 that the country was in worse condition than it was when we had arrived there nineteen years earlier. We were horrified at the accumulation of wealth by Mobutu's family. They drove Mercedes Benz cars while the majority of the people had to scrimp to get by. Graft and corruption were mind boggling."

Nancy Warlick's warrior instincts were activated by the situation. She began writing letters. "I wrote many, many letters. I also met Senators Sam Nunn (Georgia) and David Boren (Oklahoma) when they came to Zaire in 1988. The U.S. ambassador, William Harrup, took me to the head of the receiving line when the senators visited, and told us we could 'speak Georgian.'

"I told Senator Nunn that military aid was not what was needed in Zaire, and that Mobutu was skimming money off what the U.S. was sending. 'Mrs. Warlick,' he said, 'I believe you're right.' 'I know I'm right,' I said, and he asked me to keep him informed.

"At a reception the next day I gave him a packet of materials about good things the United States had done—in which the Presbyterian church was very much involved—in Zaire. He seemed very impressed, and went home and started working against military aid to Zaire. By 1990 he and others had persuaded the U.S. government to stop giving military funds to Zaire."

The next step was to concentrate on getting the dictator-president out of power, in order that the people could have self-determination.

"When we came home after being evacuated in September 1991, I began to speak out clearly. In fact I was quoted by the *African News* newspaper as saying Muboto is evil. The editor of the paper had called our daughter to see if she knew a missionary who would speak about things in Zaire. Elizabeth told him, 'My Mom will.'"

Not only that. She has testified in Washington about Mobutu. "I have to say that my testimony really made the circuit among members of the Congress and their staffs. I guess they didn't expect missionaries to talk about those things; and I came to believe also that missionaries and the Presbyterian church have a lot of credibility."

She testified in the Senate Foreign Relations Committee's Subcommittee on Africa on November 6, 1991, saying bluntly that "President Mobutu must be urged to make a swift and immediate exit and the United States must publicly break its ties with him . . . the years of Mobutu's rule have produced utter hopelessness and despair for the poor citizens of that wealthy land."

She added, among other points: "There will be no change until he is gone. . . . For twenty-six years the United States has poured more than a billion dollars of overt aid into Zaire for the support of Mobutu and his regime. . . . The United States is playing a role which has dangerous and deadly consequences for our friends in Zaire."

Thirteen days after her testimony, the House passed House Resolution 238, "in which they asked for everything I had asked for in my testimony." The Senate later passed a similar resolution .

"In March (1992) Senator Nunn wrote James Baker (secretary of state) and Brent Snowcroft (national security advisor), who had to be moved if we were to cut ties with Muboto publicly. Later in March, President Bush wrote a letter to Mobutu, telling him he had to get serious about the democratization of Zaire. In May a State Department official admitted to me that we had forced them to change their position.

"That's how I found out that in diplomacy you have to move one person to move another, to move another."

She is quick to say that her battle for the people of Zaire has been helped by many people. Thirty-four other Presbyterian missionaries signed a letter with her, asking the help of a large number of U.S. senators. "I've had many, many Africans tell me I'm right on target, and many Presbyterians have encouraged me in this journey." Reflecting on her efforts, she says, "Maybe one of the best gifts I can give those I love in Africa is to speak out in Washington."

And she is impressed by the success of evangelism in Zaire, despite the hardships there: "It has been incredible to us that, in a time of such suffering and pain, people are turning to Jesus Christ."

Both Bill and Nancy Warlick understand that their presence in Zaire would create problems as long as Mobutu is in power there. Nonetheless, she hopes they can return, at least for a visit. And, "We could very well be going back to Africa to live; we haven't ruled that out."

Betty Moore 🐝

Betty Moore was the first woman elected an elder in the John Calvin Presbyterian Church of Florence, South Carolina. "When that happened," she says, "a very dear and influential woman in the congregation said to me, 'I don't think you ought to be doing that; we have plenty of men who could be on the session. But I will pray for you.'

"I think that attitude has slowly changed," says Betty, who went on to become the first woman moderator of her presbytery,* and—on what she intended to be a brief interim basis—the first executive of Presbyterians for Renewal, a prominent evangelical organization.

In each of those cases, she remembers, she prayed a lot before agreeing to be part of precedent-setting actions and went ahead with the conviction that she was doing what God wanted her to do.

Doing what God wants is a phrase that comes up often in her conversation, and it figured in an early career decision: "During a youth camp when I was in high school, I felt that

God wanted me in some way to prepare myself for Christian service."

The Presbyterian Church in Sikeston, Missouri, where she grew up, was on the corner in the block where she lived, but it closed, "so we were not Presbyterian in the sense of having grown up in a Presbyterian background. I grew up, therefore, in a church with a congregational background, called the Church of God. It was a warm church, which developed one's personal faith and involvement. I'm immensely grateful for the background we got there: in understanding that faith is a commitment and a relationship with God, and that to feel excited and emotional about faith is very acceptable. It was not a charismatic church—but one in which faith is taken very seriously."

Sensing a call to serve God in a direct way, she turned down a music scholarship and went to Anderson College in Anderson, Indiana, a school related to the Church of God. She went on to teach sixth graders in the stockyards section of Denver,Colorado, then into guidance work in a junior high school in Denver while studying at night for her master's degree.

"After I got my master's, some of us read in the paper that military recruiters were coming through and we decided if we were ever going to travel, this was the time to do it. We went to see the recruiter. I signed a civil service contract for two years. Three of us were sent to Japan to set up a civil service guidance program for Air Force dependent children."

She was assigned to Tachikawa Airbase, near Tokyo, and sometimes sent children in need of health care to a nearby infirmary where Ralph Erskine Moore, Jr., was serving.

Erskine Moore's parents had been Associate Reformed Presbyterian missionaries in Pakistan, before his birth, "so we had similar backgrounds."

They dated for two years. She was scheduled to be transferred to France, and he was to return to the United States to complete his medical studies. "I eventually made the decision not to go to France, and went to Memphis State University where I taught for a year and he entered his residency. At the end of that year, we decided marriage was what God wanted for us and we wanted for each other."

After he completed his residency, they moved to Florence and, as in other places they had lived, became active church members. In 1969 another time came when they had to decide what God wanted them to do.

"I was with child—significantly with child—when Erskine came in one day with a letter, and said, 'What do you think of that?' The Presbyterian Church U.S. was seeking a surgeon to go to Korea and serve in a leprosy hospital for two years, while the doctor who was there came home to finish his orthopedics training.

"We prayed about it, and it became very clear this was something we should do.

My husband is very different from me in his thought processes. His theory is, 'Is there a need? Can we fill that need? Is there any clear reason why we should not fill that need?'

"It was a wonderful two years. One of the things we had to say was that we couldn't go until the baby was two months old. Erskine was commissioned while I was still in the hospital with the baby.

"It was a marvelous experience in a totally different culture. While we were there, I taught the children—Ralph his first and second grade years, Billy his kindergarten. In addition I taught English, using Christian materials, to a group of Korean federal prosecutors and judges who wanted to learn English.

"We came back home, back to the same town, in 1972."

Betty did a variety of things mothers did in that era. "I was volunteer Victoria—Girl Scouts, reading tutor, den mother, house mother, room mother at school. Taught a youth Sunday school class. When small churches couldn't get missionaries to come speak to them, Erskine and I would do that."

Then another decision time came.

"The First Presbyterian Church of Florence was absolutely furious with the developing feminist movement, so they made an appointment to talk with representatives of what was then COWAC (Council on Women and the Church). They called me and said, 'Would you be moderator of the meeting?'

"We went. Frankly, some pieces they presented at the meeting were extraordinarily good, and some didn't make sense. There was a good exchange. I think maybe some folks began to understand that they were not in good relationship with the majority of the women in the pew in the Presbyterian Church U.S. And, I think that some of the women in the congregation saw aspects of using the gifts of women that began to broaden their vistas.

"The resources coming out of the PCUS women's work did not resource the majority of women in the denomination, and did seem to speak more to advocacy, sometimes militant, roles; and even those who favored advocacy were turned off by the tone of what was going on. We can look back and see that most of those people have changed their minds."

When she was asked to be a candidate for moderator of presbytery, she recalls,

"I said, 'I don't know Roberts' Rules of Order. That's not my gift. If being moderator means I go around and be pastor to pastors and people, that's okay.'

"I was told, 'Don't worry. The only meeting you'll have to moderate will be the Spring one. We won't have any problems.'

"That was the meeting at which two congregations came and asked to be released to the Presbyterian Church in America. And I had to cast the deciding vote, to allow one to leave and not the other."

It was about that time that the Covenant Fellowship of Presbyterians, an organization** made up of members generally described as conservative evangelicals, asked her to be a member of its board of directors.

"I teased them, and said, 'You finally awoke to the need to have a token woman on your board.'

"They said, 'God forbid you should ever be a token!'"

She agreed to be a director and found the organization's work attractive: "A heart for service, doing things the national church for whatever reason didn't or couldn't do, like youth ministry, and the Wee Kirk ministry. Also, lay renewal ministry was very active."

It was a similar story when she was first asked to stand for nomination as a member of the General Assembly Council, following Presbyterian reunion in 1983.***

Delicate balances had been reached regarding representation of conservative evangelical elements and "it was decided that there would be two each from North and South added to the council. When Randy (the Reverend J. Randolph Taylor, co-chairperson of the reunion committee and moderator of the first General Assembly following reunion) called me, I said, 'I can't do that. I'm not a process, procedures person.' But after some conversation it became clear that Randy couldn't appoint controversial people, and I eventually decided to accept." She was a member of the council from 1983 to 1987.

Not long after reunion a new organization including members of nearly all the conservative evangelical wings of both former denominations came into being—Presbyterians for Renewal. Betty was summoned again.

"They asked me to be the executive for the first six months. I said, 'Don't be silly.'

"But I talked with Erskine and we prayed about it. I had the sense I was not God's person for it."

A subsequent conversation involving three ministers—the Reverends Kenneth Hall, Harry Hassel, and Clifton Kirkpatrick—helped change her mind. "Ken said that 'this is the sort of bridge we need between the past and the present.' They affirmed that I should do what I had thought of as a negative, and challenged me; they said they believed this (my taking the job) could be very helpful."

Presbyterians for Renewal is what Betty Moore calls "a new definition of the renewal movement," with a sixty-member board of directors including fifteen from the former Presbyterians United for Biblical Concerns (from the former

United Presbyterian Church); 15 from the former Covenant Fellowship of Presbyterians (from the former Presbyterian Church U.S.), and 30 "totally nonaligned." A third such group, the Presbyterian Lay Committee, Inc., from the former United Presbyterian Church, had chosen not to be part of the new renewal body.

Permeating all she does is a sense in Betty Moore's mind that the church is in the midst of exciting and decisive times.

"I believe," she says, "that we're living on the tip of a real reformation explosion. I believe the PCUSA will be a part of it. And as funky as it sounds, I believe there is a Satan, who is attacking the church.

"I believe the reformation and renewal are going to come from the congregations and presbyteries. I see some exciting and vital congregations all across the nation. The presbyteries do have ability and vision to change their ways of operating, to draw in and incorporate the new paradigm of ministry in which a lot more partnership is necessary.

"I think our generation has an assumption that when a commitment is made, it is for a lifetime, and these younger generations don't have that understanding of commitment. They see commitment in relationship to the specific positives for their lives, personally.

"I think the church is not going to be going on forever in the machinery of the past. That's strongly evident in any aspect of life. We're seeing the younger generation church-hop:

"'Whatever speaks to what I need today is where my commitment is.'

"I see that, for instance, in the church's insistence on high liturgical worship. There are numbers of people, young and old, for whom that is very significant, but when that is the worship form to the exclusion of praise music and Scripture music, there's a falling away."

The sense of a call to be involved in such times, she concludes, "was the basis of what I thought was a six-month term as interim executive of PFR. So, these years later I am continuing, but I see a definite end to it in the not-too-distant future."

She recalls that not long ago something she said left the impression with the organization's directors that she intended to leave the job in 1992, period. But her longtime confidant and prayer partner knew perhaps better than she.

"One of the directors understood it like that, at least, and said something to Erskine about trying to persuade me to stay.

"My husband told him, 'I believe she's where God wants her, for a while yet.'"

---

* At the time, Pee Dee Presbytery; the area now is part of New Harmony Presbytery.

** The Covenant Fellowship of Presbyterians was made up basically of members of the Presbyterian Church U.S. Similar groups, including Presbyterians United for Biblical Concerns, consisted largely of United Presbyterians.

***The reunion brought back together the southern-based Presbyterian Church in the United States, and the northern-based United Presbyterian Church U.S.A. The two groups had divided in the Civil War era.

❦ Caroline McKee

Like many other Presbyterians, Caroline McKee is not a lifelong member of the Presbyterian church. Although she was born in Pittsburgh, Pennsylvania—where Presbyterians are counted in multitudes—her family moved to Connecticut when she was 6. Presbyterians were and are scarce in Connecticut. Almost as scarce as in, say, Montana.

The family attended a Congregational Church in Connecticut in her grade school years. They moved later to the Albany, New York, area where "the nearest church was a Methodist church and I ended up being confirmed a Methodist as did my brother, Phil." (Philip Gittings is now a Presbyterian pastor). Another move took them to Dunkirk, New York "and we went back to a Presbyterian church—it was my Dad's choice, and wherever he went, we went."

It has been the church of her choice ever since, including in Miles City, Montana, where she and husband Fred McKee have lived since 1974 and where their children were born.

There is no great sense of the national Presbyterian

Church (U.S.A.) in Miles City and in Montana. The fact is particularly apparent to Caroline, who was a commissioner to the church's national meeting—General Assembly—in 1991. "There's no great sense of national anything in Montana," she says. "Not government, or anything. Remember, some of the original Montana homesteaders are still alive. History is short out here—one lifespan. Historical ties that are seen and felt so strongly in the Northeast don't exist out here. And the idea of anyone coming in from an urban area and even beginning to expect to tell Montanans how to live—they don't want any of that at all."

She is thoroughly involved in the work of Yellowstone Presbytery—an area perhaps two hundred times larger than the Presbytery of Pittsburgh, but with about a fourteenth of its members.

And shrinking. "We're losing about two hundred members a year in the presbytery," she reports, even though the First Presbyterian Church of Miles City had shown a small gain in membership in 1990. "Lots of people are moving out of the state; lots of jobs are moving, as companies leave.

As in other parts of the country, "Young people are not joining; it's not automatic, as it once was. And, older people are dying. The staunchest supporters of the church are getting quite old now.

"However we didn't do it, we didn't instill a sense of the church—how good it can be, what a strong support system it is—into our children. My children don't like to go to church; they don't know why they have to get up on Sunday morning when their friends don't.

"And I don't know what to do about it.

"I see out here the best way for the church to grow is through young adults. They're the people we're drawing into our own congregation, more than the younger people."

It is sometimes difficult, she finds, to be Presbyterian in an area where Presbyterians are so scarce.

"It's not easy pulling things together. There is a deep camaraderie in the presbytery arena, and I have worked in that since '82, when I was presbyterial president. When we get together we're very intentional to enjoy each other and to do the things we have to do. But in the interim times, when we don't get to see our good friends—and a lot of my best friends live one hundred fifty miles away in Billings—it's not always easy. You don't find the support in the geographic area that you'd like to have, and as a result we sometimes get kind of sloppy in our Presbyterianism.

"The pioneer instinct is strong and the population so sparse, if you want something done you very often do it yourself. That's sometimes detrimental to the connectionalism of the Presbyterian church."

Adding to that problem, she is convinced, is the strong attitude of self-reliance: "We will help absolutely anyone who needs help, but we will *never* ask for help."

Caroline had been elected an alternate commissioner (delegate) to the 1991 General Assembly and had not expected to attend it. Then the person elected unexpectedly had to undergo surgery, so Caroline was among the six-hundred-plus voters in the church's annual meeting.

She remembers her participation in it as "hard, physically draining."

To a degree, "I felt part of it all; but I also felt terribly frustrated at points by the use of *Robert's Rules of Order* to cut off debate; by not having the opportunity to share thoughts that should have been shared. I know that you can't go on and on, that debates must be limited, but boy, there were things that should have been talked about more, things that would directly impact work in the congregations."

All commissioners are members of Assembly committees that do much of the preliminary study and make recommendations on issues before the body. She was a member of the committee that dealt with a much-publicized report on human sexuality. She says the committee work went well, although in committee and particularly in plenaries, "Trying to keep up with where we were in the papers was really terrible.

"I found the videotape that was issued (to help commissioners prepare for the meeting) to be very helpful, to give us clues about ways to organize the reams and reams of papers.

Our synod does have a training day; but our synod offices are in Denver, and it's a $600 airline ticket to get down there and come back, so we don't participate in that much, just because of the expense involved.

"I spent a lot of time reading the materials.

"Also, a couple of people called me. One person called me about the church growth report, and asked that I read that. She had been on the committee that wrote that report and said 'Will you please be sure to read it.' I did, and felt it was one of the really important things we dealt with.

"The celebration of the Brief Statement of Faith was great fun. There was supposed to be a committee meeting (of the Committee on Human Sexuality) at that time, but a lot of us asked for time off because it was such an important thing to be a part of. That was a really historic moment, I felt.

"And I think the church growth report also, with the commitments that were in it for every governing level of the church, will have a direct impact on the congregations. More so than the sexuality report; but the sexuality report just overshadowed everything and that was too bad."

What does Caroline McKee think about the future of the church, locally, regionally, nationally?

"I think the church goes on, in spite of what we try to do to it. The Presbyterian church will continue to reform, and be, we hope, better every time. The church doesn't always make the greatest of decisions, but as we continue to try to make good decisions, and trust God to guide us, I think we have a good future.

"I think the mass communications that they are developing, and the computer systems and the like—of which I'm totally ignorant—are going to connect us better than we've been in the past, to some of the resources and people who are really wonderful workers in the church. I love the national staff people that I know; they're very helpful in giving us whatever we ask for, as best they can with their resources. So that will help the church.

"The loss of membership is a concern, but we're cyclical. I feel that in the not too distant future, we'll have a group of young people coming up who are once again independent thinkers, and bright, and willing to study. And if we can help that study be directed into and out of the Bible we'll have a stronger church, maybe than we've had in the past. But it will take a lot of work on the part of us middle-agers to do that. It's hard. It's hard for those of us working full-time to still be full-time church volunteers. But if we persist and allow God to persist in our lives, we'll go on. I'm not worried about us dying . . . to me the most important thing is that we stay faithful. And as long as we do that, somehow God will have this church go on."

The First Presbyterian Church of Miles City, Montana, has 309 members. It is currently seeking a pastor.

Ernie Bighorn 🦋

In the late 1800s the U.S. Congress authorized certain Christian denominations to work among American Indians in sections of the then-western frontier. Presbyterians were allowed to develop churches in Minnesota, the Dakotas, and Montana.

"Our family, along with the Red Eagle and Red Bear families, got involved early and established the Red Eagle Memorial Presbyterian Church in northeastern Montana, on the Fort Peck/Assinniboine Reservation," according to Ernest C. Bighorn, Jr.—Ernie to some of his friends and To To (Blue Eyes) to others. "That's what they call me when I go home." Home is the Fort Peck Reservation, where he was born in a government hospital, a third-generation Presbyterian.

Ernie Bighorn doesn't get home as often as he might; he works long hours at the Indian Development and Education Alliance (IDEA) he formed in 1975.

Its purpose? "The main thrust is to get Indian people and their families to live in an environment they can control."

He has a master's degree in Indian education from Arizona State University and still regards himself as a professional teacher—"a teacher by trade." Teaching is what he does, though his classroom is big and hard.

He taught high school and elementary school, then at Arizona State in Tempe, Arizona, and at Rocky Mountain College in Billings, Montana. He was at Miles City Community College, working in a project for developing Indian community colleges on reservations, when he made a decision that has kept him busy for sixteen years: "I decided to stay here and work with Native Americans who live off the reservation."

The three founding families of the Red Eagle Memorial Church are big families and "at one time there were probably two hundred fifty active members." From the beginning, "the missionaries allowed people to maintain their language and some of their cultural things. They wrote hymnals and a Bible in their language, and so had worship in Indian (Sioux) as well as English."

The tradition of doing things for themselves may be what motivates Mr. Bighorn now. His approach is painstakingly slow and thorough, but it is also highly successful at putting people in charge of their own lives.

"Getting an education is not that difficult," he reasons. "But family, social, financial matters take lots of time away from study." So he and his colleagues work to help prevent such distractions, or to provide solutions to them when they come up.

"For example, let's say we identify a nursing student, a single parent; the average age is 30. We work with that person about five years to change the social and financial patterns of that person's life and establish new habits, new trains of thought."

Seemingly small details are important in the overall goal. For instance, "We ask trainees to keep receipts for all the money they spend. They learn to be accountable for money they get from grants and so forth, and to control their own budgets better."

Handling budgets isn't the only thing emphasized. Relationships get at least as much attention, maybe more.

"On the family part, if a trainee has children, we require the parent to do at least one thing with a child during the academic year to build relationships. It may be piano lessons or a dancing class, basketball, whatever. Ernie Bighorn's organization pays for them, to strengthen the bonds between a parent learning to be on her or his own, and the child or children who see too little of the parent during the learning years.

If child care is involved, "We require a parent to deliver the child to the day care center at 7:30 and to pick the child up at 4:30, every day. That gives the mother a chance to go to the library and so on; it gives the child a sense of consistency in what's going on."

Family ties are unusually important for people who have exchanged reservation life for urban settings. "We've had very few students who failed academically; the problems have been personal, social."

The solution: "We allow students to use the phone here (in the IDEA office) anytime to call home. Day or night. It's to help them keep from getting so lonesome that they drop out."

The success rate is amazing: "Probably 95 percent." There are people who began the program unemployed and on welfare, and are now registered nurses "who probably average $13.00 an hour."

"But it takes five years to change the whole pattern, to accomplish that. The most important thing is that we've broken a cycle.

"It's a rewarding job, to see that people have made it."

The same philosophy and practice apply in any kind of program the IDEA people undertake. And the practice of emphasizing family ties, and morale, is maintained.

"You can't spend government money to buy eyeglasses or piano lessons or basketball shoes. The money we use for these things is Presbyterian money. If a person goes to the hospital, our office makes sure they get flowers, to know that someone cares.

"Or, like buying a car battery or a new tire, in order to take a child to school—those little frustrating things." Sometimes people in his office call community people—"a mechanic, for example"—to ask them, 'can you help this person?'

"All people want to know is that they're cared about, that they're not just a statistic, but that they're individuals, trying to survive in a hard world."

Money for all this is not exclusively from Presbyterians. Some is from the Department of Labor, foundations, and other contributors but it is "mostly from Presbyterians." Even so, he estimates that "$6,000 is probably the most we ever got in a year" from any single Presbyterian source.

While all this is being done, Ernie also works with welfare departments, tribal officials, education offices, college, state, and federal officers "to try to rewrite the rules, to make them more effective." He is involved with organizations dealing with national health care issues, including a Presbyterian national committee. And he has at least two more projects under way.

One is the establishment of a Native American church or mission in Montana's largest city, Billings. "That would probably be the most meaningful work I've ever seen." He is working with the Synod of Lakes and Prairies (the Presbyterian regional administrative unit for a six-state area that includes Montana) for the establishment of such a ministry.

It may be that the urge is rooted in his conviction that the church, for good or ill, operates in a class system:

"Each congregation has its own identity. Some are made up mostly of doctors and lawyers, some farmers and ranchers, and so on. If you aren't a part of such a group, you aren't part of that structure. So not many Indian people are in Presbyterian churches. Native Americans are a society of largely unemployed people, so I guess it is a class system. I'm not saying it's a bad system, that's just the way it is. I go to church (the First Presbyterian Church of Miles City) and worship with them, but I don't belong to their society. I know it, and I can live with that. . . . Maybe (being Presbyterian) is a habit; it's all I've ever known."

Another project on which he is working and to which he is strongly committed is one designed to help Native American families.

In 1974, he has learned, 60 percent of Native American children were placed in foster care—in non-Indian homes.

"It has to do with a philosophy of how we relate to another race of people, to another culture. Lutherans, Catholics, Mormons, the state tribal social service, all of them were doing it. The approach was to take children from Indian homes and place them in non-Indian homes. Basically it's a philosophy that still exists—that it's a good idea that everybody should have an Indian child. So now we have a second generation of kids with no self-identity, no self-esteem.

"I'm working for an overture (a position statement) about Indian families.

"I think the Presbyterian church needs to support Indian family unity, to say it's OK to be Indian, for Indians to raise their own children. It's important for the church to come out and say that; it doesn't cost any money to say that."

Ernie Bighorn has been working on the statement for Indian family unity for at least three years. IDEA has occupied his time since 1975. His work with state and federal bureaucracies is never ending. Yet he shows no signs of the busy executive, no strain at being so involved in so many causes.

The question naturally occurs: How do you get it all done? When do you sleep?

The answer is matter-of-fact: "Well, I guess I do need a vacation—but I don't know when I'm going to have time."

The First Presbyterian Church of Miles City, Montana, has 309 members.

❦ *Janet Hall Graff*

"One of the first words I learned to spell was Presbyterian," says Janet Hall Graff. "I have this memory of lying in bed at night, my father sitting on the edge of the bed and helping me learn it. I'm sure I wanted to learn how to spell it as an attempt to learn what Presbyterian meant.

"I remember that once I finally learned to spell 'Presbyterian', that was a great achievement. I'm not sure it helped in understanding it at all, at that age, but I thought it would." And with a pause and a chuckle she adds, "I'm still trying."

Small wonder that she tried so hard and started so young. Janet Graff was born into the church; both her parents are Presbyterians and her father, now retired, was then a Presbyterian pastor.

And were her parents born Presbyterians as well?

"No, Mama was raised in the Christian Church (Disciples of Christ), and Daddy was a Methodist and his family had been for generations. But when my parents were at the University of Illinois, they began attending the McKinley

Foundation. Daddy started helping out there as a student assistant, but actually he went halfway through law school before he found out seminary was where he was supposed to be. That calling was nurtured through McKinley, I think. So he went from Illinois to Union Seminary in New York. His father was an attorney and a judge, and that's what he had grown up knowing."

After doing her own growing up in manses, Janet went to the Presbyterian-related College of Wooster. "Of course I'd heard about it all my life. I applied, I guess, to three different Presbyterian schools—Centre, Macalester, and Wooster— and a couple of other non-Presbyterian schools. Wooster's the one that felt right. I'm not sure whether it was because of its being Presbyterian or other intangible things. Both my sisters followed suit and went to Wooster."

"I'm married to a Presbyterian who was reared a Presbyterian; his parents are both elders, as are Steve and I."

Steve Graff works for the College Board, the people who do the SAT tests, in the organization's regional offices in Evanston, Illinois, where the Graffs and their two children live. They are members of the Northminster Presbyterian Church in Evanston.

A lot of church work goes on in the Graff family. Of her own activities, "I did have a stint on the pastor nominating committee four years ago, which I found fascinating," says Janet. In 1990 she was a teacher in the sixth grade church school class. When she was on the session, she was chairperson of the Christian education committee and that background led to her being asked to be part of a family ministries committee, "coordinating some of the activities that come under the Christian Ed umbrella but are more focused on families." Both Janet and Steve help in "driving kids to choir rehearsals and that sort of thing."

Janet does some freelance calligraphy—"at my own pace, partly because I tend to find myself busy enough doing volunteer things—church, PTA, swim club, so that I'm not sure I'd have time to do anything else. I imagine I will work at some point as the kids get closer to college age, but I've felt it important to be home with them and think that's made a difference. And I feel fortunate that we've been able to manage it."

What keeps her a Presbyterian? "It's funny, but I can't imagine being anything else. I've done this Presbyterian thing all my life and it makes sense for who I am at this point. I haven't had reason to be dissatisfied with it, which I think is why a lot of people leave the church, or change, or look elsewhere. So far, it seems to fit in.

"I think part of that has come from being involved at a variety of levels, in different places. We have a sense of that connectedness that seems to be coming back all the time. I think some folks don't always get that sense; but there's been a richness about it, in how it manifests itself in the people who are involved, in the varieties of liturgy and worship experiences; I think that keeps it alive and not so staid that you go through the motions but become disaffected by it."

She has not been alienated by the disputes over some of the church's positions and programs. "I guess I expect there to be controversies, and see that in many cases as being helpful. Some of it goes with the idea of being in a church of people who always seek to be educated, too; that's part of the education process, having controversies and discussions and working through things—and coming to a consensus on occasion, or agreeing to disagree sometimes."

She thinks of involvement as an important component in the denomination's future, as well as of its present:

"A lot of people miss out on being what 'Presbyterian' is by not having a wider view of the church. Some of them don't even know what a presbytery is. There needs to be some contact and education. I think too many people tend to look at the church nationally only when there's something controversial going on, or when there's a big fund-raising program, and they miss out on so many things. Just educating people about Ghost Ranch and the other conference centers, for example, or synod schools, trying to get them involved, would be a start. To have more people subscribing to *Presbyterian Survey* would help. People in our own congregation have been surprised sometimes to learn that such a thing exists."

She recalls that Chicago Presbytery has sponsored "training days" for new session members and deacons. She found the one she attended to be interesting and instructive—"but again, events like that tend to be only on the officer level, and what happens doesn't filter down too much."

Despite the shortcomings, "There's a sense of family in the church. You can be in a group and start talking, and the connections start popping up all over the place. Twice, just in Evanston, we've moved next door to the children of Presbyterian ministers my father knows. Twice, within eight blocks of each other. That's part of the richness, too."

Those things, she believes, also are part of what makes the church unique in all of society:

"I like to think that I wouldn't still be with the church if it didn't mean something to me; and I've seen enough in my own life to believe that there's really something to all of this that we've been talking about all these years. The faith that I see people living, and how things are manifested in people's lives—there are just too many coincidences not to believe it. Not just in my own life and spiritual development, but witnessing this in other people, too; in their being agents for change and good work. I've seen it happen. And it keeps me there.

"But to get back to the original question of what makes this church unique, I think it's a combination of tradition and flexibility, openness to new things, but still maintaining a sense of history.

She cites an example connected with the Graffs' first, recently acquired, piano: "We've been wanting one for years and years. Just after we got it, Mama and Daddy presented us a copy of the new *Presbyterian Hymnal,* and we sat there around the piano, flipping through the hymnal. There were both the old and the new, hymns my family has been singing over the years, and the new ones we've learned together or that each of us had learned separately. There was a lot of history just wrapped up in that hymnal, so that it seems completely appropriate to have it be the first set of music for our new piano. It was a nice way to christen the instrument. It was just the right gift, right then."

The Northminster Presbyterian Church of Evanston has 930 members. Its pastor is the Reverend Jeffrey S. O'Neill.

Abraham Hsu

How Abraham Hsu came to be a Presbyterian is a long story, but the reason he remains a Presbyterian is simply stated: "I never thought of being anything else."

He was born into a Lutheran family, in a church compound in China where his father was a pastor associated with a Norwegian missionary society. Abe lived there until he was 19.

By the time he was graduated from high school the Communists had taken over his native land. All schools had been closed. "I was trying to decide what to do," he remembers, "and I went to stay with my sister in Hong Kong." The borders had been closed by that time, but the closing was not yet seriously enforced. He went to college there for four years. Meanwhile, his sister's work took her to Thailand, to the Bible Training School (now the Bangkok Institute of Theology) operated by the Church of Christ in Thailand, of which Presbyterians are a part. Following college he rejoined his sister and taught in the training school, "working with missionaries from several denominations; Presbyterians were predominant."

After three years, "Presbyterian colleagues, the Reverend and Mrs. Clifford Chaffee, recommended me for further education in Princeton Theological Seminary, through the (former) United Presbyterian Church's Commission on Ecumenical Mission and Relations." Margaret Flory and Betty Parkinson, who were doing student work for the Commission at the time, were instrumental in his pilgrimage:

He attended Princeton Theological Seminary for two years, then transferred to Union Theological Seminary in New York City for a degree in religious education. Upon graduation he returned to Thailand. "I went back to the same job, but then they made me dean of the school." He was ordained to the ministry by the Church of Christ in Thailand.

In a Thai language class he met Anna Stevens, a Presbyterian missionary nurse who had been sent to the country a few months earlier; they were married about a year and a half later. "After our first child had arrived, we went back to Union and Columbia University." His career led on to service as an assistant pastor in Troy, New York, and student work at Rensselaer Polytechnic Institute and Russell Sage College. He served seventeen years as associate pastor of the Faith United Protestant Church in Park Forest, Illinois, before he joined the staff of Palisades Presbytery as associate executive presbyter and moved to Ridgewood, New Jersey.

There are three Hsu sons now—James, studying creative writing, Kenneth, a mechanical engineer, and David, who works in Milwaukee, Wisconsin. Abe has two brothers in China and one in this country; his sister, now retired, also is in China.

Abraham Hsu believes the church that has so thoroughly affected his life is in a very difficult time, in complicated circumstances. He cites an illustration used by the Reverend Clifton Kirkpatrick, director of the denomination's Worldwide Ministries Division, about the comments of a Kenyan pastor who was introduced to decaffeinated coffee: "It looks like coffee, it smells like coffee, and it tastes like coffee, but it doesn't have the punch and power of real coffee."

"I've seen a good many Christians who lack the punch and power," Abe adds. "That seems to describe the Presbyterian church's situation."

From his vantage point as an official in a middle governing body of the church, he describes the difficulties like this:

"Membership has been going down (in his geographical area) in the last twenty to twenty-five years. The high cost of housing means most younger families can't afford to stay there. Population demographics are top heavy with older people. The church somehow is not reaching younger people.

"In my presbytery nearly every church is going through some kind of financial difficulty. Even in those with substantial endowments, giving is not what it should be. And the local church causes come first.

"I don't see any evidence of a turnaround in my presbytery. The reasons are complicated. I don't think Presbyterians train congregations to do evangelism and do it well; every time you mention the word, there's an argument over what it means.

"Most people in the pews don't know or care what the denomination is doing. The only time they hear about it is over controversial things, and those things stick for a long time."

But he is not about to give up.

"My wife's family were very traditional Presbyterians—her grandfather was a pastor, and her father an elder. It never occurred to us to go elsewhere. Besides, the Presbyterian church is not any worse than any other," he says with a chuckle.

Summing up, he says this: "I tend to take a long term, historical view. Even though it's going through difficult times, the church has always gone through problems, and the church survives. I try to see it with eyes of faith; I see that God is doing something in spite of us.

"History is not in our hands. It's in God's. What we have to do is be faithful to our calling.

"In the end, that's what keeps me going."

🍒 *Bruce Stinson*

When Bruce Stinson was born, the Indian Trail Presbyterian Church was a comparative youngster itself—less than two dozen years old, with a building that was a bit younger still.

He was baptized there as an infant and joined it as a full member at age 12, six decades ago. It is the only church, the only congregation, to which he has ever belonged.

In an era when mobility is the norm and most Presbyterians began their church life in some other denomination, small wonder that some of his friends call Bruce Stinson "a dyed-in-the-wool Presbyterian."

The Stinsons live about a mile from the church. In his life of membership there, he has "done about everything in the church except preach." He has served "I don't know how many years" as a deacon; he is ordained a ruling elder and, since the rotation system* went into effect, has "only been off for about a year at a time." Along with other such responsibilities, he has been Sunday school superintendent, and a member of the Stewardship Commitment Committee and the Property and Grounds Committee. He's been a commissioner to presbytery several times, but hasn't been elected to any synod or General Assembly responsibilities.

"He didn't have time for that," Mrs. Stinson volunteers. "We had three children to raise, and he was a working man."

But he has found time to be at worship services regularly, as attested by a sizable collection of perfect attendance pins. "They've given me pins for perfect attendance for forty-six years, but that's not really honest; they allow you to miss four Sundays a year. But I never miss more than four Sundays."

Bruce Stinson's work was that of a diesel truck mechanic. He began with the White Motor Company, which later became Lucas Truck Sales. He worked forty-two years, twenty-three of them as a Mercedes truck mechanic, before retiring in 1987.

Bruce's mother was Presbyterian but his father had been Lutheran before their marriage. The parents became charter members of the Indian Trail Presbyterian Church when it was organized in 1913. The building, still in use, was completed in 1915. A rock veneer was added in 1935.

"The members hauled rocks for the veneer from fields, some that had been blasted out in a road project.

"Originally they didn't have stained glass windows. My daddy got the windows started. His cousin agreed to pay for the first windows if my daddy would install them. He put in two in the chancel, plus a Stinson family window in another part of the church. Other members did the rest."

The church—situated in the community of Indian Trail but with a Matthews, North Carolina, mailing address—grew to about three hundred members. But "About five years ago there was a fight and the membership is down to about two hundred now. A certain group got it in for our preacher, and got him out. The only thing I could ever really find out was that they were too liberal and couldn't get him to go by their lifestyle. We had a voting for him in the church; eighty-six voted not to accept his resignation and thirty voted against him. He chose to leave; he said he couldn't take it anymore."

The disruption "lasted a good year or more." Hard feelings have lingered.

Mrs. Stinson, leafing through a history of the congregation, counts up and finds that the church has had twenty-one pastors—fourteen of them installed, the others as supply or interim pastors—in its seventy-eight years. Mr. Stinson adds that it was part of a three-church parish once, but has been self-supporting for at least the past twenty-two years.

He reports that "We give to overseas mission, and help a missionary: Alice Hester, out of this congregation. They ask that we give a certain amount of our budget for mission." Mrs. Stinson adds that the church has furnished meeting space for an Alcoholics Anonymous group for twenty-five years or more, and "for Brownies and all sorts of Scout troops."

Bruce Stinson can recall a time when men and women sat separated in worship services. "When I was a boy, all the men sat on the left and the women on the right. It seemed like the young people (he gestures, spreading his arms then bringing his hands together) started sitting together in the middle.

"Worship wasn't as formal as it is now; there wasn't as much of a pattern."

And although he doesn't oppose change in all things, he doesn't necessarily favor it, either. He chuckles, reflecting on the reaction of the Reverend George T. Lashley, the present pastor, in one such instance:

"The Session voted a while back to change the Sunday School hour from 10:00 to 9:45. I told them, 'This church has been having Sunday school at 10:00 since 1913, and I don't see any sense in changing it.' George thought that was funny."

Despite the differences over the previous pastor and the resulting drop in membership, Mr. Stinson finds the Indian Trail Church to be "Pretty solid. It's going to be slow recovery, gradual, but I think it will be steady and solid."

As for the church as a whole, his outlook is more conditional:

"I feel like it may continue to dwindle down, unless we have a disaster or something to bring people back. When times are good, people forget. When hard times come, they call on the Lord."

* A rule limiting the consecutive number of years—usually six—a person may serve on a church board.

The Indian Trail Presbyterian Church has 190 members. Its pastor is the Reverend George T. Lashley.

❦ Harold Nettles

It is easy to think about the Old Testament story of Job when listening to Harold Nettles—although the comparison is far from exact and is one he would never make. Nevertheless, much like Job, he had an ample share of this world's goods, and like Job he saw it systematically taken from him.

And like Job, he never stopped trusting God.

Harold Nettles of Douglasville, Pennsylvania, was a partner in a company called CryoChem Engineering and Fabrication, Inc., making a comfortable living and looking toward retirement when his own set of calamities began. In brief, this is what happened:

The partners had arranged to sell the company and had come to terms with a buyer when the Environmental Protection Agency (EPA) entered the scene. Tests showed that extremely small amounts of a commonly used solvent from the CryoChem manufacturing plant had leaked into the area water supply. State and federal government agencies began looking for ways to correct the situation, at the partners' expense.

The cause of the trouble was a compound used to test the quality of welds on products manufactured at the plant. "We had switched from another compound to this one when we learned the first one was a danger to the environment," Harold explains.

"We had no idea there was a problem (with the second compound); we learned about it after some had seeped into water wells. When we learned about it, we stopped using the product immediately and hired an engineering firm to monitor it."

Step by step, they were caught up in a maze of government bureaucracy.

"No one ever came and said, 'You've got a problem.' In the very beginning, if they had told us (about the problem), we could have put in filters in all the wells for about $40,000." Harold subsequently supplied water to the fourteen homes in the area where underground water was affected.

"We never denied anything; we worked with them 100 percent." The government wants the partners to pay $1.3 million for a study of the damage.

"There's nobody you can talk to." He estimates that the company is "worth a couple of hundred thousand dollars." He and his partners already have spent $285,000 in the matter and they face another $745,000 in future losses.

Long before all this happened, Harold had a pond built in front of the manufacturing plant. Trout were raised in it, and with them he stocked streams in the area. He makes no mention of that, however. He only says, "I've tried to be an environmentalist my whole life. Even as a kid. I'm looked upon, evidently, as a polluter . . . and this hurts more than the money."

Harold and Hazel Nettles's doing of good deeds has been a lifelong habit. Much of it is centered in Pottstown, a city of about 28,000, near their Douglasville home of forty-five years.

They were Lutherans "until about 1972" when they switched to the Presbyterian church "because we thought there was more opportunity to do something" for people there.

In the late 1950s Harold had been part of a program "whereby fifteen to twenty white people and an equal number of black people would get together and study black-white problems. The idea was that after two years of training these teams would go out and try to help solve the problems." But carrying out the idea was not well received, and the church terminated the program.

Although "the Lutheran church has changed tremendously since then," Harold has long since become deeply involved in Presbyterian activities.

"I've been interested in Christian mission work all my life," he says, and when pressed offers a litany of such involvements:

- He was instrumental in getting the Pottstown school district to hire its first African American superintendent, "and we got at least one other black on the teaching staff. I guess we were like gadflies; we kept the school district aware of minority problems."

- "I continued working on black-white problems in Pottstown, to bring about better relations, especially in the schools."

- About four years ago the Cluster of Religious Communities, an organization similar to councils of churches, opened an outreach center in Pottstown providing food, clothing, furniture. He was secretary of the cluster for five years and has been "deeply involved in other cluster activities over the years."

- In housing, he was the founder and longtime president of the Interfaith Community Housing Corporation in Pottstown, organized in the mid-1970s. "We tried to get funds to build low income housing in Pottstown, and were close to getting a government grant when the government pulled the rug out from under housing projects." Even so, "about five years ago, with money that had been accumulated, a pastor in Pottstown rejuvenated it and they have rehabilitated a number of houses."

- He has been coordinating the CROP walk in the Pottstown area for seven years. The annual walk, to raise money for world and local hunger projects, involves "about eighteen churches and two hundred fifty walkers." It gathers $8,000 to $9,000 a year to fight hunger.

- Despite the unpopularity of opposing the Vietnam War at the time, he spoke out strongly against it.

- Hazel and he "have been pushing the church to make facilities for handicapped people available"— and they have succeeded; such facilities have been installed in the First Presbyterian Church of Pottstown where they are members.

Why does he do all this?

"Well, I have a deep commitment to God. Even though I have problems, I've lived a good life, comparatively speaking. I've never been rich, but I've experienced so many events, and I've really been fortunate that my health has held up relatively well. I can put myself in the place of people who have lost hope."

Work in the Outreach Center has been particularly important to both Harold and Hazel. "Volunteers there probably derive more satisfaction than the people who come in for service. Hazel and I each put in about forty hours a week in it.

"If it weren't for that, this EPA problem probably would have had a more serious impact on us. It affected our physical and mental health, and created problems between Hazel and me . . . but in the past couple of years we have been closer than ever."

The loss inflicted by government agencies is a heavy weight. "We paid our people more than we ever took out of the company. I thought the world of everyone who worked for me. I started by working in the shop, so I knew what they had to do.

"After giving the best part of your life and looking forward to retirement, to lose everything is a shock. That our government would penalize us like this is unbelievable."

Given the nightmare he still is having to go through, does he ever get the feeling God has forgotten him?

Quickly: "No." And at that moment Sheri, a handsome and friendly collie, walks up to him to be petted.

"We've always had collies," he says, patting her head. "The last one we had died, and we got a phone call from a kennel; they were looking for a good home for a four-year-old collie. Sheri has taken to me. I was feeling so low when we got her; it's as though she came from God.

"I haven't given up on God. No; I thank God every morning when I get up and every night when I go to bed."

William Winter ❦

William Forrest Winter, Democrat, was elected to the Mississippi Legislature when he was a 24-year-old law student. He went on to become the state's governor in 1980–84.

In many ways his career in public office was only the beginning of his career in public service.

Bill Winter, private citizen, created a foundation to seek solutions to economic, educational, and social problems in a three-state region. He has given time to causes ranging from mental health, education, and freedom of information, to historical societies, election law reform, and the Bill Clinton presidential campaign in Mississippi. He is co-author of three books, has headed the Appalachian Regional Commission, and has been a trustee of Columbia Theological Seminary, Rhodes College, and the Southern Center for International Studies—among other activities

In a long list of involvements and honors on his biographical record from the Mississippi Department of Archives and History is also the entry: Elder, Presbyterian Church.

Talk with Bill Winter and you don't hear much about honors and accomplishments; he is not given to boastful use of first-person pronouns. Instead he talks of ideas—of what is involved in the art of politics, of the principles that have guided his political career, of what can be accomplished in such a career. And of the faith that has shaped his values and his beliefs.

The forming of his faith began in Grenada, Mississippi, where he was born, and where his parents and their parents were Presbyterians. "There's a window in the Grenada Church in memory of my great-grandfather. His name was William H. Winter. He was one of the early leaders of the church; he had come to Grenada County in the 1830s, so it was in his lifetime that the church there was organized.

"As long as I can remember, I've been going to Sunday school."

Does the church—the denomination—of the 1990s look different from the one of his boyhood?

"Obviously, it has the same elements as those that have sustained it through the years—the belief in the fundamentals of our religion. But obviously what's different is the very substantially changed culture in which we live, with a much more complex social dimension to it. And, I would have to say, there are many more problems that test the generation of my children and grandchildren much more severely than I was tested. I grew up in a rural environment, on a farm, in a much simpler time, when the choices of how we lived and how we conducted ourselves were much less complicated and much less ambiguous than they are at the present time. As a result of all this, the role of the church, it seems to me, is a much more complex role, and is a much more challenging role, than the one in which I grew up in the Grenada of the 1930s."

He attended public school in Grenada, too, graduating as valedictorian of his high school class. He went on to the University of Mississippi for B.A. and LL.B. degrees and was named the outstanding law graduate there in 1949.

World War II interrupted before he finished his law studies. He entered the infantry as a private and advanced to the rank of captain, serving in the 86th Infantry in the Philippines in 1945–46.

Was it tough duty in the infantry in the Philippines?

"It promised to be even tougher duty. I actually did not see combat in World War II (he later was recalled to active duty in the Korean War in 1951). I spent most of the war training soldiers for infantry service. But I was sent overseas in the summer of 1945, ostensibly to be in an infantry division that was scheduled for the invasion of Japan; so when the atomic bomb was dropped in the summer of 1945, it probably saved my life.

"I spent a year in the Philippines in the mopping up and rehabilitation work."

How does he feel about the use of the first atomic bomb?

"I thought it was the right decision at the time. Undoubtedly it saved many lives, Japanese as well as American lives. It was estimated that the invasion, if it had been carried out as planned, would have resulted in perhaps 500,000 Allied casualties. So I have always felt that President Truman made the right decision, given the situation he was confronted with. Since that time, I have felt that we must diminish the risk of any use of nuclear weapons, because of the proliferation of those weapons and the terrible casualties that would result from the use of them."

His career in politics began with his election to the legislature a year before he got his law degree. His political involvement has continued, along with strong convictions about how faith and politics interact. "I think faith says the same thing to me as a politician that it says to anybody else; I don't put politicians and public officials in any different category from people in other vocations, other activities. Faith provides a stablizing set of values that, I think, gives one in politics—where there is frequently a certain ambiguity, a certain ambivalence—a sense of what is proper, what is right. I think one's faith is important in sorting out the real issues."

Some Presbyterians feel that the Reformed tradition almost requires that people be involved, not necessarily in politics but in the life of the community. Does that say anything to Bill Winter?

His answer is quick, and plain: "It's what I was raised to believe."

He was reelected to the legislature without opposition for two more terms and resigned to accept appointment as state tax collector. Elected to another term in that post, he determined the office was an unnecessary one and requested, successfully, that the legislature abolish it. He was elected state treasurer in 1963.

He ran for governor in 1967 and lost because of his position on civil rights.

Were the civil rights days tough for a man with beliefs such as his?

"They were," he says. There is a long pause.

"I was in the middle of the political arena during that whole period from the late forties to the early eighties. I grew up in a segregated society, in a society where no thought was given to any other way of life than a segregated way of life. I came back from World War II having served in a desegregated infantry unit, recognizing that there were changes coming. I didn't know just what form they would take and how long they would take, and to my dismay I saw the lines being drawn pretty tightly, particularly after the Brown decision* in 1954, the rise of the massive resistance movement and the White Citizens Council, and with the hysteria that dominated the deep South in those days.

"So it was with difficulty that one in politics was able to avoid the kind of fatal confrontation that would end one's political career, at the same time that one did not succumb to the hysteria.

"For example, I was told that if I didn't join the White Citizens Council, my political career was over. Well, I never joined the White Citizens Council. And I never took a position in politics where I consciously used the race issue to advance my political image. There were times when I didn't say anything; but when I did say something, I tried to make it a constructive statement.

"And then as the hysteria mounted, we had the confrontations of the early 1960s, which I suppose reached their climax with the Meredith riot at Ole Miss,† I became increasingly vocal in calling for a different approach that recognized that white people had to change their attitudes, and we had to embrace the adoption of processes that ensured that people could vote, and have protection of their basic rights. I became increasingly a spokesman for that point of view, and it cost me my first race for governor."

He opens his desk drawer and takes out a leaflet distributed in the 1967 gubernatorial campaign. "I keep this in my desk just to illustrate the kind of race I was confronted with. It was a flier my opponent used, showing black people in my audience and saying that if I were elected, black people would dominate Mississippi. I lost that race. I came back later, of course, to win (the 1980–84 term) but 1967 was a mean race."

"In 1971, I still had a campaign debt from my 1967 race and thought it was premature to run for governor again." He ran for lieutenant governor and was elected.

"Then I ran for governor in 1975 and was favored to win, but I got caught up in a unique political situation where a populist came along and adopted a gimmick that just captivated the people. Instead of campaigning in a conventional way, my opponent would spend each day working in a different occupation, with television cameras covering him. It was such a novel approach that people got caught up in it; he was 'one of us.' He was shown driving a bulldozer, driving a gravel truck, cutting pulp wood, sacking groceries in a store—a different occupation each day. It swept the state and I got snowed under. I was defeated in a race I was favored to win, defeated by the largest margin that anybody had ever lost by, in a second primary in Mississippi.

"I thought I would hang it up after that, but this fellow had such a bad record that many people who had voted for him indicated they would support me. I really hadn't intended to run and literally at the last minute, sixty days before the first primary, I announced and was elected by the largest margin by which anybody had ever been elected governor. So things turned around for me, which is another lesson I learned in politics: sometimes being in the right place at the right time is important."

At that time Mississippi law provided for a single, four-year term as governor. The law since has been changed. He ran for the U.S. Senate the year after his gubernatorial term. "It was not a very good decision. I ran against a popular incumbent, who was a Republican, in a year when Ronald Reagan was running for reelection. So I was defeated in that race."

Win or lose, are his religious beliefs a driving force in his dedication to service through politics?

"I think so. Again, without taking myself too seriously, I think the basic values that motivate us in our everyday lives are also involved in why and how we face political decisions. In my case, those values are grounded in what the church has taught me in its many manifestations—through its influence on my parents, my teachers, the people I grew up with, as well as through the formal structure of the church itself."

His support of good causes, especially those involving education, goes back to his time in the state legislature. As a state representative he was the primary sponsor of the state's workmen's compensation law, and was instrumental in the passage of the Minimum Foundation Education Program in 1954. As lieutenant governor he backed further education programs, and others designed to aid elderly, handicapped, and underprivileged people. He was an outspoken advocate for opening the processes of government to the public and the press, before open meetings were in vogue, and received an Associated Press Freedom of Information Award for such efforts.

Is he satisfied with what he was able accomplish in public offices, especially as governor?

"I don't guess we're ever satisfied that we've done as much as we wanted to do. But I'm pleased with the Education Reform Act (passed in 1982) we were able to push through. It raised teachers' pay, created public kindergartens in every school, and established school attendance laws—Mississippi had no compulsory school attendance law. It also set up accreditation of teachers and schools based on performance. It was recognized as the first comprehensive reform act in the nation and served as a model for other states."

Does he have any desire to be back in public office?

"Not to run for office. I'm still active in the party and participate in a lot of political activities, but I never intend to run again, myself."

But not running for office is, for Bill Winter, far from being idle. Since leaving office he has been chairman of the National Commission on State and Public Service, the Commission on the Future of the South, and the Kettering Foundation; served as a trustee of the Southern Association of Colleges and Schools; headed Youth Leadership Jackson; and is president of the State Department of Archives and History.

One of his major post-gubernatorial projects is called the Foundation for the MidSouth. He helped establish it, and helped accumulate $3 million to fund it. Its purpose is to identify and link up with successful programs, and launch new ones, that provide homes, jobs, and hope to people in distressed counties in Arkansas, Louisiana, and his home state. The law firm in which he is a partner—Watkins, Ludlam, and Stennis—lends it office space.

He also spearheaded the Bill Clinton presidential campaign in Mississippi, "along with Congressman Mike Espy, who is a black congressman from Mississippi and a fine, fine young man." He was cochairman for about a year, although he had other key roles much earlier."Bill Clinton and I have been very close friends for a number of years, and I was one of a small group of people who met with him in Washington before the campaign ever started, to participate in the decision that he would run. Of course we started at a time when nobody thought he would get the nomination, and certainly nobody thought he would beat George Bush or have a chance to beat George Bush."

Is there something about politics that gets into the blood?

"Well, I think there is an attraction to it. There are lots of frustrations about it, but I think those go along with almost anything one does. I think the chief attraction lies in the opportunities it affords for one to get to know, on a fairly personal basis, so many of one's fellow human beings from all areas of society.

"But more than that, without taking oneself too seriously, you have the best opportunity I know of to use politics as the basis to make things happen in a community or a state or a nation—and, depending on one's approach, to make things happen for the better.

"I don't know of any other area of human activity where one person or one small group of persons can make a greater impact than in the political field. Because, ultimately, the political decisions that somebody has to make—that determine how life is lived in this country, how communities are organized, how basic services are provided, the quality of education, the answers to concerns about the environment, whether we kill each other or not in war—the basic questions of human existence ultimately boil down to political decisions."

What about the future of the Presbyterian church in such a world?

"I feel good about our denomination. It has come through some very difficult times that have had, I think, too much emphasis on that which has divided us and not enough on that which unifies us. It is a denomination, I think, that has continued to speak prophetically to the broad spiritual issues of our times, sometimes with resultant misunderstanding and confusion among some of our members; but I have felt that what the church is supposed to be about is to express, and continue to search for, the truth that will lead us to the creation and maintenance of a society where peace and justice and concern for our fellow human beings, regardless of who they are and what they look like and where they live and what socioeconomic condition they're in, will be paramount."

*The Brown vs. Board of Education case in which the U.S. Supreme Court ruled against "separate but equal" facilities, and ordered integration in public schools.

†James Meredith was the first black student admitted (1962) to the University of Mississippi and entered the school amid much hostility. He was shot and injured in June 1966 while participating in a civil rights march in Mississippi. Race riots broke out thereafter in a number of cities including Chicago, Cleveland, and New York.

❦ Rebecca Sue Gander

Rebecca Sue Gander, who marked her 28th birthday in October 1991 has been a Presbyterian all her life. She is vice president, loan operations, at the Lincoln County National Bank in Stanford, Kentucky. She is mostly known to friends as Becky.

She began working at the bank ten years ago: "I was two months out of high school, and started in the bookkeeping department and worked my way up.

"The bank is going to change its name to the First Southern Bank; it'll be part of a small chain of banks. I'll still have my same job."

The Presbyterian Church of Stanford is where her parents (both now deceased) attended, where she was baptized, and where she was confirmed at age 13.

Becky is not an officer in her home church, but not because of lack of opportunity. It is because she simply doesn't see herself as a leader—at least not yet. She has been asked to be an elder, on at least two occasions, but has declined.

Why? "I feel I'm too young, to be perfectly honest. I don't feel like an authority figure. Even in my work I have a hard time dealing with that. I'm mostly a follower, instead of a leader. If I had accepted the nomination and been elected, I would have been the youngest person to be an elder in our church, the first who wouldn't have been at least 50 years old, or at least in the late 40s."

Would she ever agree to serve as a church officer? "Possibly. I wouldn't rule it out, but I don't feel like I would be the right nominee. I think the elder position is more power than I'm ready for."

That doesn't mean she's not an involved member. She has been singing in the choir since she was in the seventh grade, and has been teaching in the church school for a decade. She has served two terms on the worship committee and one on the evangelism committee. She is a part of a circle made up mostly of women her own age, using Bible studies prepared by the national organization of Presbyterian Women. On occasion she types the session's minutes and the deacons' report, and she regularly prepares the Sunday bulletin.

Her hometown is approximately one hundred miles from Louisville, Kentucky, where the national offices of the Presbyterian Church (U.S.A.) have been situated since 1987. That doesn't make a lot of difference to her. She doesn't hear much about the church as a national body, and doesn't read much of Presbyterian publications. "What I do hear is generally from people in Sunday school class who do read the papers," says Becky. "Our minister is our Sunday school teacher and people will come in and say, 'Well, I read that this is what all Presbyterians believe now; the church has taken a stand on this'—and then there'll be a big discussion on that controversy or situation and Ray will have to get everybody regrouped. If I didn't hear about it in Sunday school, I probably wouldn't hear about it."

Nonetheless she thinks it's good to have the church's national offices reasonably nearby: "I think most people around here are pleased to be as close as we are. If we had something we needed to get from Louisville, we know people in those offices now. If I really needed something, I feel like I could call . . . (But) If we needed anything, we would have a tendency to contact our minister and it would be his job to go further with it."

She is concerned, but certainly not ready to give up, on the future of the congregation that is so much a part of her life.

"I see it decreasing," she says. "I see people moving away, as young people go away to college and take jobs in other places. It's hard to replace people. But I don't see it as a lost cause. I intend to do what I can, anyway."

As for herself, "I feel I'm a very firm Presbyterian. I visit lots of churches, but it's easy for me to say that I will always be a Presbyterian."

The future of her home church and the whole church could be helped by the same thing, Becky Gander believes:

"What the Presbyterian church here and the larger body needs may be training in evangelism. We need to have a good jolt to our spirits. We need some excitement.

"I heard a friend in Sunday school telling about a senior in high school who said he attends two different churches. On Sunday morning he goes to the Presbyterian church for his educational growth in God. But as far as being spiritually energized, he goes to the Baptist church on Sunday nights. He said he felt he needed both.

"I thought that was kind of sad."

The Stanford Presbyterian Church has 119 members. Its pastor is the Reverend R. Lee Jennings, Jr.

Ben Keys 🍒

Ben Keys says of himself that he is a "dern near unique brand of Presbyterian."

He was a Baptist by birth—"it's tough to grow up in Greenville, South Carolina, and not be Baptist"—but he went to an Episcopal boarding school for high school classes. He describes the change as going "from a very narrow minded view of religions into a relatively sophisticated culture."

In that environment for four years, he says, there was heavy emphasis on the Bible. "And I learned a lot about the Episcopal church."

Then, "unlike a lot of other folks" he went to the University of North Carolina at Chapel Hill. He says he "found I didn't need the church" but in his freshman and sophomore years he attended a neighborhood Episcopal church with a buddy although "it was a little stiff for me." He went to Unitarian and other churches, and even took a course in religion during a summer term at Furman University, back home in Greenville.

"I floundered," he says now. But: "I was drinking beer with a buddy when he said, 'I don't believe in God.' And I said, 'I believe you're crazy.'"

From the University of North Carolina he went into the Navy and was shipped to the Middle East. "I found that when there was a worship service on board, I'd wander back to it. I guess I liked the music."

After the Navy, "I came back all pumped up with confidence and really didn't need the church."

Despite that new conviction, when he got married—to a Presbyterian "they would say on Sunday mornings, "Which church do you want to go to?" They started attending an Episcopal church "but every Sunday morning I had to introduce myself" to the pastor. "My wife being Presbyterian, we said, 'Why don't we go to the Presbyterian church?' We tried several and landed in the small Fourth Presbyterian Church. It felt comfortable. After our second Sunday visit there the pastor showed up at our house and said, 'Glad to have you there.' And we've been there ever since."

The couple eventually had four sons and thought the youngsters should go to church. "We were pretty strong there in the ten to fifteen years the boys were growing up. The preacher there fit my style." And, as always happens to Ben, presently he was asked to serve on the church's board of deacons, later on the session, and on a pastor-seeking committee.

Along the way the family acquired a summer home in the mountains that changed their churchgoing markedly.

"Ten or fifteen minutes from that house is an ecumenical chapel with a little of all of the above, including a different preacher every Sunday. They asked me to serve on the board over there."

None of those experiences has made Ben Keys into an every-Sunday churchgoer. "My mode right now is that I am obsessed with the mountains, and have become a wildflower fanatic. I love the outdoors and usually am there every spare minute, with my camera."

In 1990 they bought a larger place not far from their original mountain home—and this one is winterized. "Sixty-five acres of the most beautiful land, with a beautiful trout lake, and secluded. The home has heat in it so we're up there every week."

They go to the services in the ecumenical chapel every Sunday in the summertime.

Meanwhile, back in Greenville, Ben "got hooked in here with a men's breakfast group"—from twelve to twenty-five men who meet every Friday for breakfast and talks by various people—"and I never miss that."

Given his checkerboard experience with the church, what does the church do for Ben Keys? He answers readily: "The Presbyterian church as such and its beliefs are not important to me. I couldn't articulate the differences between denominations." But: "I consider myself to be relatively intelligent and logical, but I haven't been able to find the answer to what makes us tick or the universe go. I have to believe in a supreme being.

"I still have a lot of unanswered questions but it (faith) has given me strength and belief in the hereafter. I haven't been able to find anything else that provides that strength."

Has the Presbyterian church done his sons any good?

"The jury's still out. But I'll tell you what—I hope and pray for those boys. I think, given their own choice, you wouldn't find any one of them in church. They go when they're home, for their mother and grandmother. But they would probably get something out of it. I hope we (the church) have given them roots they can attach themselves to and grow forward from. I think they're good boys. They have higher standards than most. I think the church did them some good, gave them roots to find good soil and good water."

Has his own belief changed any over the years? "I'm not sure it has changed dramatically, so much as my faith has matured and strengthened. At age 53, I know I need help and somebody to lean on, more than I knew at 23. A friend of mine said, 'As I get older, I get more spiritual and less religious.' I agree with that.

"Presbyterians, Baptists, Episcopalians—none of those denominations means anything to me."

But they are still members of Fourth Presbyterian in Greenville. "And if I were here on Sunday, I'd be there."

The Fourth Presbyterian Church of Greenville, South Carolina, has 663 members. Its pastor is the Reverend Allen McSween.

Robert Long 💕

The story of the Reverend Robert G. Long could almost be a story about a classic case of clergy burnout.

He spent more than four years on the staff of a large church and left to develop an upscale church in a "new town" outside Chicago. Spurred by an integration problem in the community and in the congregation he was serving, he became heavily involved in the civil rights movement of the 1960s.

One day, tired, he turned his back on the ministry. He bought a dairy farm and milked his first cow. He became a truck driver for two and a half years, then worked in the management offices of a large truck dealership.

Somewhere along the way his name was placed on the inactive roll of Chicago Presbytery. About the same time his marriage started heading toward a divorce.

What makes his story something other than a history of burnout is that nearly a dozen years after he left the ministry, he took his ordination vows again and became pastor of a small urban church with a future that is, at best, iffy.

Bob Long finished seminary training and was ordained in 1956. He was a military chaplain for two years. Then he joined the staff of the First Presbyterian Church of Fort Wayne, Indiana. That was followed by five years in the new church development project in Elk Grove, Illinois, and a year doing administrative work at McCormick Theological Seminary in Chicago.

Then "I took a kind of sabbatical for eleven years," he says. Because of burnout? "Yeah, although I didn't identify it at that point."

What he did identify was that "having gone through a time as a fairly active participant in trying to bring about peaceful integration, I just got kind of tired, worn out." When the assassinations of John F. Kennedy, Martin Luther King, Jr., and Robert Kennedy occurred, "Some kind of energy and hope died in me . . . I felt like it was time for myself and my family to regroup."

Involvement in matters of integration had started in Elk Grove when a black couple applied to buy a home in the developing suburb and the developers would have preferred not to sell. The administrator of the suburb came to Bob Long for advice, "and I said to him, 'If you want a lot of negative publicity, turn them down.'"

Changes took place rapidly after that. A Human Relations Council was organized and Bob persuaded a Roman Catholic priest to be its president; the black family eventually moved in and enrolled their daughter in a Roman Catholic school—all "with minimal problems."

Bob walked in the landmark civil rights march from Selma to Montgomery, Alabama, as a representative of Chicago Presbytery ("scary; a profound experience for me"), and took part in other work on behalf of racial justice during the tumultuous years of the late sixties and early seventies. "I got lots of psychic energy in that era; but that takes a toll on you."

His family—a wife and two children at the time— was "very supportive of me" in the period. They had relatives who were interested in owning a dairy farm, and decided to try that occupation. But five years later, "having discovered a phrase called 'return on investment'," he got out of the dairy business. "I drove an over-the-road truck for about two and a half years, from St. Louis to New York to Knoxville; that was my basic route." Among the unlikely experiences of that period, he remembers an afternoon when "I parked my semi-trailer rig on the campus of Princeton (New Jersey) Theological Seminary and went in and had a talk with (then-president) Jim McCord."

Sundays when he wasn't on the road he attended the Presbyterian Church in Edwardsville, Illinois, and on occasion helped with the communicants' class. A student intern asked him if he'd like to preach. He said, "Sure" and his journey back into the formal ministry began.

"I became a kind of temporary supply preacher. They wanted me to become their pastor; I had to wait six months, because of the rules, and then retook my vows, in Eliza Parish, Lovejoy (now Giddings-Lovejoy) Presbytery."

Later he was a pastor in Wood River, Illinois and an interim pastor in north Minneapolis before going to the Andrew Riverside Presbyterian Church in Minneapolis.

"When I first got there, about forty to forty-five people would be in church on Sundays; most of them older persons who were the children of Scandanavian and East European immigrants. And there were three families from Ghana, including one whose ancestors had been converted three or four generations earlier by Scot Presbyterian missionaries."

One day, Bob recalls, one of the Ghanian members told him some friends from Ghana wanted to have their baby baptized. I said, 'Fine,' and asked him, 'How would they baptize the baby back home in Ghana?'" That's what we did.

"The word went out, and a lot of Ghanians came to worship that Sunday. In the baptismal rite the minister lifts the baby up overhead three times and says, 'Lord bless (baby's name) and keep him.'

"People saw that we honored the customs of our brothers and sisters in the faith, and so we had lots of baptisms. We always baptized one baby at a time, unless there were two or three in one family." Typifying the diversity of the congregation, "One fall the first three baptisms we had were of Neal Nicholas Nelson, the second was Jamal Bodom, and third was Kyung Hwan Kim.

"We had to learn the difference between inclusiveness and integration."

Did being pastor to such a congregation give spark to the life of Bob Long?

"Oh, man!" he replies, and is propelled into more stories about Andrew Riverside.

"One Sunday we had an all-African service of worship, with the sermon in an African language and that wonderful African music that ended with us tapping our feet to it. In their (Africans') music, joy comes out of a profound faith and hope that God's gonna win.

"We had a Ghanian funeral that was exceptionally moving, including a drum farewell. One of our members was here getting his master's degree in ethnic musicology and is a master drummer. Somebody would make a statement about the deceased, then the drummer would repeat it with the drums."

The congregation is now about one-third Ghanians, one-third baby boomers, and one-third sons and daughters of Scandanavian and East European immigrants. But it is still small and its future is uncertain.

Describing the situation in the early autumn of 1991, the pastor said:

"The reality is that this is a church that probably is not going to be able to make it financially; I probably am not going to be able to be their full-time pastor much longer.

"It gets somewhat scary when you look down the line. We've been kind of preoccupied with survival, and we're trying to turn that around and be preoccupied with ministry. I'm 60 years old, and I wasn't in the Presbyterian pension plan for those eleven years." But his face lights up with another thought about the goings-on in the congregation he serves, and it is plain that Bob Long is far more concerned about Andrew Riverside's future than with his own.

"Our morale is good. And where else can I have the privilege of relating on a daily basis with people from Scandinavia, Zaire, Africa, Korea . . . ?

"The miracle is that much of the leadership and energy at Andrew Riverside Church is being provided by grandsons and granddaughters of nineteenth century African converts—so mission has come full circle in Minneapolis, Minnesota."

In November 1991, the Andrew Riverside congregation determined it could no longer afford a full-time pastor. Typically, pastor and people celebrated Bob Long's last Sunday there in a worship service that included gospel music, Ghanian drums, a sermon on "Dreams and Visions," and a solo rendition of John Lenon's "Imagine" by a member who formerly had lived in a halfway house for chemical abusers. A football practice jersey, bearing the name of Cincinnati Bengals quarterback "Boomer" Esiason, was presented to the departing pastor by a representative of the neighborhood street people. In September 1992 Bob Long became interim pastor of the United Presbyterian Church of Washington, Iowa.

The Andrew Riverside United Presbyterian Church in Minneapolis has 121 members.

❦ Bob Wilson

You might say Bob Wilson is successful at everything except retiring.

He worked in radio for thirty-one years before quitting, but is back at it with his own five-times-a-week program. And he began his third stint as choir director for the First Presbyterian Church of Sheridan, Wyoming, with the understanding that "I'll do it if you'll keep looking" for a successor.

He is a slight, gray-haired, soft-spoken man whose appearance belies a storehouse of enthusiasm and energy. Sitting at a coffee shop table in Sheridan he recognizes and is recognized by nearly everyone who comes along. Ask him about either church or radio and he is ready to talk—or do—on a moment's notice.

Both radio and church careers began early. He was working in a retail store in the World War II era when "A high school friend called me and asked, 'what's your draft classification?' I said, '4-F.' He asked if I wanted to get into radio. I told him I knew nothing about radio. He said, 'If you're 4–F, I can teach you radio.'"

Before his full-time radio career was over "I did everything but (sports) play-by-play," Bob remembers. "I did do color commentary for ball games, and I even was a third class engineer." However, "I didn't get into news until I came to Sheridan in 1949."

His news hawking began when he became concerned that the station's newscasts were so limited. "Daily, someone would come from the paper with a summary of the news. I didn't like that and suggested trying to get news for ourselves. The boss said it was okay 'If it doesn't take away from your time' on other duties.

"Our news became very competitive. When I quit radio in 1973, an editorial in the paper said, 'Bob Wilson is out of our hair and we're going to miss him.'"

Bob began directing the church choir in an emergency when, "in late 1949 or early 1950" a job transfer sent the previous director to another town. Bob stayed in the emergency job until 1969. A series of other directors came and went, and then he was asked to take up the task again.

Music has been a love since high school days; his love for the Presbyterian church came a while later.

"I grew up Northern (American) Baptist and was very involved in young people's work—state president of the Baptist Young Peoples Union" and such. He was at an international youth conference in Lakeside, Ohio which was "the first time I had ever been exposed to activists—a total awakening." The event centered mostly on racial causes, he recalls, and jolted him because "out here in the West we weren't very much aware of the social gospel."

On graduation from high school he began working with a youth group called G and G, for "Guys and Gals." In addition to Sunday school they had a weekly social: "The kids contributed a nickel a night; I went to bakeries and dairies and got food at cost, so we were solvent.

All this was in Billings, Montana, his birthplace. After their marriage, Leila and Bob Wilson were living in Miles

City, Montana. Leila's father had been a Methodist minister; and the newlyweds were visiting various churches. "We went to our respective churches," Bob recollects, and found "they just weren't warm and comfortable."

Then one Sunday, while "shopping around," they went to a Presbyterian church and decided to join. "We told the pastor we were interested in becoming part of the work of the church." The pastor was the Reverend John B. Fitz, "a very vital" minister.

"He suggested we try starting a young people's group. We called it 'Guys and Gals' as in the earlier group; the pastor suggested we try that in private, but in public, 'let's call it Grace and Grit.'"

Bob remembers devising a ritual—"this was before the days of inclusive language"—that went, "As a member of G and G, I recognize my responsibility to God first, the other fellow second, and myself last."

Is this Bob Wilson's philosophy? "Oh, yes!"

Along the way music had been very important to him. "I was taught by a very fine choir director, took vocal music in my school days." He also directed a biracial—white and Native American—group, and led community choirs of up to seventy-five or eighty members.

But his twin passions have not been exclusive ones. First Church Sheridan, organized in 1904, was housed from 1911 in a downtown building. When the congregation decided in the late 1970s to move to a new location, Bob was made chairman of the committee to pick a site.

"I began totally neutral" on where the new building should be. Later, though, when the eventual site had been chosen, "I went out and walked it, and fell in love with it."

The congregation moved into its new home in 1979.

The new church building is an element in another project that was a source of much satisfaction to him.

"At the annual meeting of our church members in 1986, each proposal for some new program or project had been countered by the contention that new obligations should not be incurred until the mortgage had been paid off on our new facility. The balance was $49,000.

"In the closing minutes of the meeting, a member couple expressed disappointment that we were willing to be stagnant, just because of the remaining debt.

After the meeting Leila and I went over to them and asked what we were going to do about it. We all sat off to one side and came up with an idea.

" 'Forty-Nine in Eighty-Six' provided the opportunity for forty-nine individuals or families to pledge $1,000 each beyond their regular giving, to be paid at the time the forty-ninth such pledge was made, before the end of the year. If the goal was not reached, no payment would be asked and we'd return to the status quo. The four of us started it, and we were surprised that most of the others wanted to do the same."

But disappointment was ahead. "At the close of the year the campaign—complete with a progress chart, published reports, and announcements—had resulted in only twenty-nine pledges. So the chart was taken down and the announcement was made that 'Forty-Nine in Eight-Six' had failed.

"Then a funny thing happened. Voluntary contributions came rolling in and on the first Sunday in February 1987 a man handed me a check for $1,000. The debt was paid."

In between other involvements Bob has been on the session* "a couple of times," is much involved in the use of symbols in the church, arranges flowers for the chancel, and works closely with pastor Ted Tromble in taking care of details such as lighting in worship services.

What has kept Bob Wilson in the Presbyterian church for fifty years? The answer is quick and not surprising:

"They use me. I can always be of service."

*Governing body of a local Presbyterian church.

The First Presbyterian Church of Sheridan, Wyoming, has 450 members. Its pastor is the Reverend Ted Tromble.

❦ Herb Kirk

In the summer of 1991 Herbert Spencer Kirk entered three events in an international track and field meet in Finland. He won gold medals in two of them—the 800 and the 5,000 meter runs—and finished second in the 200 meters.

Herb Kirk was 95 years old at the time.

"When I'm in a race, I'm in there to run my very best!" declares Mr. Kirk, who is not much more than five feet tall and surely doesn't weigh more than 120 pounds. The determination that marks his running is descriptive of his life.

As a Lehigh University student he was too small for football or basketball so he took up wrestling and became a member of what he recalls was "a very good team."

He volunteered as a Naval aviator in World War I but later met some Germans, thought "Why should I want to kill those people?" and became an ardent pacifist until the rise of Adolph Hitler caused him to modify his views.

After he got out of the Navy he worked his way up the corporate ladder in a pottery firm, then accepted an offer to operate another one, making fine dinnerware "where there was an opportunity to use your interest in design." The return of English and Japanese pottery makers to the field after World War II heightened competition to ulcer-making levels. It was at that point that his wife, Eleanor Lois Kirk, told him, "I think it's time for you to get out of this." He agreed. Her father was ill and needed someone with him, anyway. So they moved to her hometown of Bozeman, Montana where they've lived ever since.

But retiring from business did not mean retiring from the world or from the zeal of living in it. Along with running and other activities, Herb Kirk for the past ten years or so has been teaching Native American students at Montana State University the art of pottery making. He also carries on a long—and thus far frustrated—campaign with the Bureau of Indian Affairs to establish a pottery making program for residents of the depression-ridden Blackfoot Reservation.

Herb Kirk was born in New Castle, Pennsylvania and met Eleanor while he was on a sales trip in California where she was a student at the University of California in Berkeley. She was a lifelong Presbyterian; he had attended the Episcopal church but became a Presbyterian when they married. He was 29; she was 20.

Both have been busy in the First Presbyterian Church of Bozeman. She has served as a deacon, has taught Sunday school, and "belongs to a ladies' group." He sang in the choir until it was hard for him to read the music, and when asked to be an officer he chose to be a deacon instead of an elder because "I felt I could do more that way."

It was in his term as a deacon that he became superactive in a housing program. "We've always had good ministers here," he says, and one of them "had an idea about getting into a community housing program." But there was less than unanimous agreement with the minister's style. A split developed in the congregation. "Some were for him, and some against," Herb says. "The congregation voted by a very narrow margin to keep him but the presbytery decided there was too much opposition, and he left."

Of his own role, Herb recalls that "I was slapped on the wrist a little bit for taking the church into the community too much. What I was doing was going to people with large houses and trying to get them to split up their houses to take care of college students. I was asked to stop. I did. I stopped my active participation in the church."

After that experience does he still feel the church ought to be engaged in such projects?

"Oh, very strongly so. Get out in the community, be a part of the community."

And of the world. "I wish the church would do more in international affairs. I strongly think the church should take a stand."

It is clear that Eleanor and Herb Kirk are still stalwart members of each other's fan clubs after more than six decades of marriage. But that doesn't mean they always agree, or hesitate to say so. On the subject of international affairs and his change from pacifism to supporting an adequate United States defense, U.S. actions in the recent Gulf War come up as an example. Says Herb: "We straightened that out."

Quickly and quietly Eleanor replies: "No, I don't think we straightened it out at all!" And with a mutual chuckle their conversation moves on to other topics.

Herb has been running since fading eyesight forced him, in his late 80s, to give up his "rather strenuous" tennis game. "A friend got me interested in running and I became fairly good at it. I won quite a few medals in my age bracket."

Eleanor went along to the International Veterans Track and Field meet in Finland—"to pick up the pieces," she says, "but there were no pieces to pick up." Instead, he was written about in *Sports Illustrated* magazine.

Mostly, however, Herb concentrates on his two projects related to pottery. He began teaching the course after learning that there were ninety Native American students at Montana State. Getting university officials' permission to offer a pottery-making course, he began what has become an enduring and popular elective. His class meets three times a week, with from nine to fifteen students enrolled.

But they are interested in making pottery as a hobby, not a profession. "They're going to be nurses, secretaries, engineers, teachers. But I like having something to do—and we do make some very nice pottery."

The head of the MSU Department of Engineering had asked Herb's help in testing some clay, about the same time that a man from the nearby Blackfoot Reservation was seeking assistance in solving the unemployment problem there. Herb, of course, got involved.

"We worked up a plan for making pottery on the reservation. Then we went to the Bureau of Indian Affairs with a request for $70,000 to start the project. The BIA in their wisdom took it out of our hands and gave it to a consulting firm. After fourteen months the consultants came out highly recommending the proposal—but by that time interest on the reservation was dead and I couldn't get it revived." But predictably, he keeps on trying.

And the Kirks keep on going to church, even though they are not as active as they once were.

The future, they believe, is going to be loaded with some terrific problems, and they hope the church will help solve them. Eleanor explains it this way: "We're not concerned for ourselves, at our age, but for the children and grandchildren. What kind of world are they going to come into? The church could play a very important role in that."

The First Presbyterian Church of Bozeman, Montana, has 547 members. Its pastor is the Reverend Charles O. Wilming.

❦ Jerry Knoblich

Jerome (Jerry) Knoblich is a teacher.

He began teaching at Jamestown (North Dakota) College in 1957, and except for a couple of years when he tested his taste for industry, he's been teaching there ever since. He is a professor, and chairman of the chemistry department at Jamestown.

When someone observes that it is clear he loves teaching, his reply is quick:

"I do. I really do."

"You get a little discouraged at times, but when you do see that success"—his face lights up and he doesn't need to finish the sentence.

Among the marks of his success as a teacher are the percentages of his students who have gone on to do doctoral studies—for M.D.s or Ph.D.s.

He is an unusually modest man. It shows in his response to the comment about his students and their doctorates:

"We are sort of proud, I guess, of our science majors. I

maybe had something to do with it, but it takes a number of people."

He adds that from 1975 through 1990, about 50 percent of the Jamestown College students with majors in biology or chemistry went on to study for doctoral degrees.

But it's not so much his record as his style that makes clear his love for his calling.

Jamestown College is growing. It is a fact that brings a tone of mixed pleasure and distress to his voice. Pleasure because he is glad the school where he has taught for more than three decades is doing well; but distress because it also means larger classes and less time to spend with individual students.

"Probably where I'm more effective is between class sessions. That's what I've liked about the college here; we've been relatively small. Had I been in a larger institution I probably wouldn't be so enthusiastic about it. Having the opportunity to get to know them (the students), I think, is what makes the difference. One of his classes in the fall 1991 term started with seventy students; the ideal size, so far as he is concerned, is thirty.

He has been teaching summer terms at North Dakota State University in Fargo—where most of his classes start with sixty or so students—and remembers an incident there that illustrates his concern for class sizes. "Three students there asked me to write letters of recommendation for them. That was rather strange; I'd only known them for five weeks. I thought it was a commentary on our educational system: all three students were from large institutions and didn't feel close enough to their regular profs to ask them for recommendations."

It was while he himself was a student in the Presbyterian-related Jamestown College that Jerry got acquainted with what was then the United Presbyterian Church U.S.A. and is now part of the Presbyterian Church (U.S.A). The way he became a Presbyterian is something he introduces as "an interesting story."

He had grown up a Baptist. While he was in high school there was "a lot of internal fighting" in the church he attended. "It made a very bad impression on me. They even had a fist fight on the steps of the church. I said, 'When I get away from home, I'll not ever set foot in another Baptist church.'

"When I came to Jamestown to go to college, I started going to a Presbyterian church and I've been a Presbyterian ever since."

His wife JoAnne had belonged to a Missouri Synod Lutheran church and chose to join the Presbyterian church when they married. She told her pastor (who now is retired) of her plans.

"When she told him she was going to become a Presbyterian, he basically told my wife, 'you're going to go to hell,'" Jerry recalls. "I felt so sorry for him."

Some years later, one of the Knoblich daughters began taking part in youth programs at the local Church of the Nazarene; she eventually joined that congregation and subsequently has done "a couple of summers of missionary work in Ireland and Guyana" through the Nazarene denomination. Mrs. Knoblich, much interested in programs and opportunities offered for young people and not satisfied with those offered in the Presbyterian church, also has joined the Nazarene church. Jerry attends services with them sometimes but has remained a Presbyterian. (The Presbyterian church since has initiated a program for youth of all ages).

He is impressed, though, with the church they have joined. "Our youngest daughter is much more—call it religious— than our other children. I really feel it's because of the influence of the Nazarene church's youth program.

"Further, local churches seem to have much more direct involvement with the national office. They have regional colleges today, and I'll tell you, their local churches really support their local college."

What keeps Jerry Knoblich in the Presbyterian church? Before health problems forced him to cut down on activities in 1986, he was "quite involved" in the First Presbyterian Church of Jamestown. He served, among other things, as a deacon, an elder, and a member of the church's education committee. In 1992 he was in the second year of another three-year term on the session.

"And I guess for one thing, we've been blessed with good pastors. For another, I really have some problems with the more fundamentalist churches, where they get very emotional. Presbyterians are generally not like that. I'm not saying that fundamentalists aren't nice people—and Presbyterians can be really somewhat cold, depending on the individual church. But I guess I'm not that emotional when it comes to religion."

Do Presbyterians in Jamestown, North Dakota, know or care much about what's happening in the church nationally?

"Lately I guess I haven't heard that much."

From his time as a session member he recollects a time of sharp disagreement over the paying of per capita fees—amounts levied by regional and national church bodies for ecclesiastical expenses.

"There was a lot of criticism over that one. It was felt, in terms of the synod and presbytery, that of the money spent to pay salaries, not much filtered down to the congregations. People wondered what they were getting out of it, and thought they would be better off sending the money to missionaries or using it for local programs. We ended up paying, but there was a lot of discussion."

As a career teacher, what does he think of the American educational system?

"I really think we're not turning out students the way we should as far as ability to read and understand and to think things through is concerned. The students have the potential, but not enough is expected of them; they're just not being pushed hard enough, not expected to do that much, in high school."

He has not had a large number of students from other countries in his classes, but has been impressed by those he has met. "The few such students I have had were much better prepared in the science areas, and in music and the arts, than the American students. This is especially true of the

German students; some of them could speak five languages and have had five years of chemistry.

"We just don't have that environment in this country that emphasizes the value of good music, good literature. Every third year the Jamestown choir tours Europe for two or three weeks. Our students notice that students of other countries are so much more interested in art, music, language, literature.

"When we (Jamestown College) were smaller, in the 1950s, we had about three hundred students and two full-time language instructors. Over a period in the 1960s and '70s we didn't have any full-time faculty in foreign languages. (By 1992 interest seemed to be on the upswing again, and there were again two full-time foreign-language faculty, but for a considerably larger student body). What in the world happened to our interest in foreign languages? Language itself is a learning tool; when you learn a language you learn something about the culture itself."

Has the Presbyterian church made a difference in his life?

"Yes, I think it has. I've found comfort over the years. At times they weren't there when I needed them most, but at times they were. When I went into industry, in Wisconsin, we were newly married; the church there was very, very good for us. There was a young couples' club and we met some very nice people. Also, there was good music and a good minister."

He had similar experiences while at Oregon State University in Corvallis, and during the time he was finishing work on his own Ph.D. in Fargo. "We liked the church there and the minister has become a . . . very good friend. In those respects the church has been valuable to me.

"If it wasn't, it was probably more my fault than that of the church itself. I was so engrossed in my teaching, I didn't work at it very hard, is what I'm saying."

The First Presbyterian Church of Jamestown, North Dakota, has 329 members. Its pastor is the Reverend Ernest C. Williams.

Agnes Norfleet 🍒

Ask Agnes Norfleet why she is a Presbyterian and her answer is instant:

"Genetic disorder," she grins.

How so?

"Both my parents were Presbyterians. My father was a minister, graduated from Davidson, went straight to Union Seminary in Richmond. When he finished the regular work he did graduate study and during that time they hired him to work as treasurer of the seminary. Later that became his full-time position, which he held until his death in 1968. I grew up on the seminary campus.

"Mom graduated from PSCE (Presbyterian School of Christian Education, also in Richmond, Virginia). Her parents were also Presbyterians. My father's father and his three brothers supported Presbyterian evangelists who worked in the North Carolina mountains. When my father was 16, he spent a summer working with the evangelists, going from place to place. His job was to spend the night in the tent where they had their meetings, and if it rained he had to loosen the ties so the tent wouldn't cave in from the weight of water on it."

At the time she was interviewed, the Reverend Agnes Winston Norfleet was in a time of transition: from associate pastor at Central Presbyterian Church in Atlanta to pastor of the North Decatur Presbyterian Church in an Atlanta suburb. Her predecessor at both churches had been the Reverend Joanna Adams, who left Central to go to North Decatur and North Decatur to become pastor of Trinity Presbyterian Church in Atlanta.

Ask Agnes why she's a minister and her answers come more slowly.

She was "very active" in the church youth group when she was in high school, and first started thinking about the ministry in those years. But there was an early roadblock: "I was chosen to be a youth representative on a committee to nominate an assistant pastor (they don't have that title any more). The idea of getting a woman for the job came up, and it was thrown out the window." She concluded at that point she didn't want to be a minister: "I decided that was a battle I didn't want to fight; I didn't want to be a pioneer."

She was graduated from Davidson College in 1981 and did two years of social work. "I hated it. I was dissatisfied, working with masses of people and not being able to help any of them individually. I wanted to do a one-to-one kind of counseling." So she eventually enrolled at Union (Richmond), still not sure what had persuaded her to go there and thinking she would like to teach or do pastoral counseling.

The call to the ordained ministry came as "sort of a gradual process over time; it happened via reflection on experiences, retrospection. I realized in retrospect that social work had prepared me for the kind of community work I do at Central."

Shortly after she finished seminary, though, she had an opportunity to serve a year-long internship in Trinity Presbyterian Church in Charlotte, North Carolina. She did preaching, teaching, and pastoral care there, and "that solidified my sense of call to a local church."

Called to the downtown Atlanta church in 1987 as its community minister and ordained there, she was propelled into much wider responsibilities when the pastor moved a year and a half later. With a chuckle she says, "I wonder how many transitions God can sustain me through. In the course of one year I got married, acquired a new colleague at Central, moved my home twice, and now I'm entering a solo pastorate." Her husband, Larry Arney, is an architect who is executive director of Habitat for Humanity in Atlanta and, in her description, "a Methodist turned Presbyterian by marriage."

Now about to begin her first solo pastorate, how does she expect to go about teaching her parishioners about the Christian faith from the Presbyterian standpoint?

"Part of my community ministry experience has been bringing people with many different experiences together with the tradition of the faith, and capturing all that in dialogue. Presbyterians historically have had social justice concerns; helping people reflect on social justice issues through biblical perspectives is not only doing the Christian thing, but also the Presbyterian thing."

She senses an increased interest in matters spiritual and intends to do something about that in her pastorate:

"While the Presbyterians have had social justice emphasis and a high emphasis on education and an intellectual approach to scripture, I think we may have deemphasized the spiritual dimension, taken it for granted. My experience in the pastorate has increased my interest in spirituality, especially as it relates to community ministry. What I have learned is that you cannot give and give and serve and serve unless you are nurtured. We do that in worship and in Christian education, but I think we need to be more intentional about it. I think that's what people are starving for in this country. We're taking it more seriously now.

"We need to find more ways to do Bible study in our churches. We cannot assume that people know and read the

Bible, or know tradition or church history. They don't always get it in church worship services any more.

"The other key task, beyond the spiritual one, is finding ways of helping people build community in a very individualistic society. People don't know their next door neighbors like they used to. People need a community—a place to process the pain when death or tragedy strikes; to share the celebrations; to nurture children."

From a young woman who "never envisioned myself as a pastor" when she finished college and "had to overcome a little shyness" along the way, she is clear and certain about it now. Asked if there is anything else she would rather do than be a pastor, she shakes her head quickly and firmly. And, after a reflective pause, says, "Nope. I love it."

"I want to be a pastor—a preacher, a teacher, a pastor in the generalist sense of the word. I think that's where my gifts lie. Beyond that I want to continue in roles of leadership in social justice concerns, and the place from which I want to do it is in the congregation.

"I love to preach. I do have a passion for it. I love the creative process, the studying, the challenge of making that ancient word relevant for us today."

North Decatur Presbyterian Church has 416 members.

Katherine Paterson ❦

Katherine Paterson was a student in the Presbyterian School of Christian Education when she was stopped in the hall one day by Dr. Sara Little, one of her professors.

"Sara—I would have called her Dr. Little then—asked me if I'd ever thought about being a writer," Katherine remembers. "I said I didn't want to add one more mediocre writer to the world's woes.

"She said maybe that's what the Lord wanted me to do—which made me realize that one has to risk being mediocre in order to learn. So that's how I got to be a writer."

Her first book was *Who Am I?*, written for the Covenant Life Curriculum of the then Presbyterian Church U.S.

"After I wrote it," she says now, "I discovered, 'this is what I love to do.'"

Seven years passed before the publication of her first novel. But eleven novels and many writing awards later, her love of writing is unabated and her joy at being able to write is just as evident.

Ask her why she writes and she answers quickly: "I'm one of those very, very blessed people in this world who found what I love to do and can do it. It's a gift in every sense. Of course (with a chuckle) if you have a gift you have to work like the dickens!

"It's a staggering thought to realize that things you write, things that come out of you, touch other people's lives. It is overwhelming—but very gratifying, to make that kind of connection with people."

She was born Katherine Womeldorf, in Qingjiang, (Jiangsu Province) China, one of five children of George and Mary Womeldorf, Presbyterian missionaries. The elder Womeldorfs went to China in 1923; the family lived there until 1937 when the country became a battleground. They came to the United States, returned to China, and were living in the riverport city of Jingjiang (Jiangsu Province) when the U.S. consulate ordered all American families out in December 1940.

"I started kindergarten soon after the war had broken out in China," she remembers. "At first they wouldn't let us go home. Later we took a Red Cross train to Hong Kong, with bombs falling all around us. We had to go to the United States via Europe. So I finished kindergarten and started first grade in Virginia, before we went back to China about a year later."

After the 1940 expulsion, "we went to Virginia and moved in with my poor, dear aunt (Anne Campbell) in Lynchburg. Here she was with her sister, her sister's husband, and their five children—and I do not remember my aunt ever being anything but funny and gracious."

Katherine finished elementary and high school at Winston-Salem, North Carolina, and was graduated from King College in Bristol, Tennessee, in 1954.

"After college I taught sixth grade in a rural school in a poverty-stricken area of northern Virginia. It was a wonderful experience for me; I had every age from ten to sixteen in my classroom. They were so great—but they were so very poor.

"The church wanted people to have some teaching experience before going to PSCE (Presbyterian School of Christian Education in Richmond, Virginia). I went there after the year in northern Virginia." She was graduated from there in 1957. Following her parents' pattern, she entered missionary work and went to Japan where she studied at the Kobe School of Japanese Language.

"I spent two years on the island of Shikoku, riding my little motor bike everywhere I could. I worked regularly with eleven pastors and taught a Bible study class in Japanese. It went fine until they started asking me complicated questions—for which my mastery of the Japanese language was not adequate."

While she was in Japan, the church's Board of Christian Education offered her a fellowship for further study. "I got to pick where I wanted to go, so I applied to Yale and was accepted. But a missionary colleague said, 'Yale used to be the place to go but now Union (Union Theological Seminary in New York City) is the place.' He persuaded me to apply there; I did, and was accepted, so then I had to withdraw my application from Yale."

The change of schools affected more than her studies: it brought a young minister named John Paterson into her life.

"While I was at Union, John was in a two-week continuing education class there. He had gone to the apartment of Robert McAfee and Sydney Brown, and asked them who knew how to play bridge. Sydney sent him to our apartment (I was sharing quarters with four other women). I didn't know how to play bridge, but that's when I met John."

The next day he asked her "if he could pursue the possibility of my marrying him." This was in February. They were married the following July, and "I learned to play bridge and tennis on our honeymoon. John taught me."

John was pastor of a church near Buffalo, New York, at the time, but wanted to do graduate studies. They moved after a year to Princeton, New Jersey, where he studied at Princeton Theological Seminary and worked part-time at the First Presbyterian Church. She taught at the nearby Pennington School for Boys.

"We had decided when we got married that we would try to adopt two children and to have two of our own. Knowing that it took so long to adopt a baby, we applied within a month of when we got married." John, Jr., was born while they were in Princeton and Lin (Elizabeth Polin) arrived from Hong Kong six months later.

Their son David was born just after they moved from Princeton to Takoma Park, Maryland, where John was pastor for thirteen years. "Lin had been saying she wanted a sister who looked like her and we had applied for another Asian child through Lutheran Social Services. We were told the agency had never placed a child of Asian birth, but they said they had an American Indian child, and we said, 'Of course.' That's how we got Mary (Mary Nah-he-sah-pe-che-a)."

After Takoma Park they were in Norfolk, Virginia, for seven years. They moved to John's present pastorate in Barre, Vermont, in 1986.

Meantime her writing career was soaring. *The Master Puppeteer,* published in 1976, won a National Book Award for Children's Literature. *Bridge to Terabithia,* 1977, (later adapted as a play) got a Newbery medal. *The Great Gilly Hopkins,* published in 1978, received triple awards—a National Book Award for Children's Literature, a Newbery honor book, and a Christopher Award. *Jacob Have I Loved,* 1980, brought her another Newbery medal.

As for those and other honors, she says, "It gets a little embarrassing." But she talks with obvious feeling about her favorite: the Janusc Korczak Award, given by the Polish branch of International Books for Young People. She received it in 1981 for *Bridge to Terabithia.*

"I went to the Polish embassy in Washington; there were five of us there. The ambassador from Poland said, 'I need to tell you about this man' (Janusc Korczak) for whom the award is named.

"He was a man who befriended gentile and Jewish children in Poland during the holocaust times, eventually moved into the ghetto with his Jewish orphans and went to the gas chamber with them. The ambassador who told us this later resigned and disappeared, as his own statement in support of the Polish Solidarity movement."

Aside from the work of writing itself, Katherine is in much demand as a speaker and is busy as a citizen. "In the children's book business you're asked to speak a lot, to librarians and school teachers. They have tough jobs, and they need to be encouraged. But I try to do no more than one speech a month out of town, and I swore off for 1993, because speaking takes so much time and concentration away from writing."

She did a lot of "tramping and ringing doorbells and telephoning" in the 1992 presidential campaign, and made her first political speech. Why all that involvement on top of her other commitments?

"How can I complain about what's wrong, if I don't do everything in my power to change it?"

Do John and the children support her in all these things?

"Absolutely. In fact, when John asked me—formally—to marry him, he said, 'I know you're a very strong woman, with gifts. And if you'll marry me, I'll help you.'

"I don't know any other man who could have stood it.

"The children? People say, 'How do the children react to your being a writer?' I answer, 'They've never known me when I wasn't a writer.' They're all very supportive."

Three of the children are married now and Lin has a daughter, Katherine Elizabeth, who marked her second birthday in September 1992 and who evokes typical grandmother stories from Katherine.

As a person born to Presbyterian missionaries and married to a Presbyterian pastor, how does she feel about the Presbyterian church?

"I love being a Presbyterian. I don't think for a moment the Presbyterian church is perfect, but no human nor human institution is. In the Presbyterian church I can be intellectually honest. I can ask questions without being ostracized. It has a rich theological heritage I can chew on.

"I love the hymns, the order. Presbytery has to be taken into account, and the session.

"I love to visit other churches. When I travel, I do, because (laughing), Presbyterian churches don't always have 8 A.M. services and that may be the only time I have free. I go to Episcopal churches, Roman Catholic ones. I love their liturgy. But I miss the Presbyterian sermons and singing.

"The Presbyterian church has given me uncountable riches. And in a very real sense it has made me who I am."

Afterword ❦

Un-Presbyterian as such may seem, this little book was never intended to be heavily serious or scholarly.

There was never any intention, or effort, to carry out an organized study by way of the conversations it records. Those interviewed were chosen, not scientifically but by an erratic combination of methods and means including time, travel, and pure happenstance. In most cases I had not met the people before. Although they come from a medley of places, backgrounds, and philosophies, the demographics of the project wouldn't be at all acceptable to a formal researcher.

The book certainly was not designed to be a theological tome—although instances of considerable theological weight frequently appear in the words of those interviewed.

So it is not a study or a survey. It is a series of conversations with randomly selected people, compiled in admiration of the work of Ernie Pyle a generation ago, and more recently that of Charles Kuralt.

But try as we may to avoid it, we Presbyterians appear destined (or doomed, maybe) to analyze. It's in our bones. We can't seem to see or hear, to read or listen, without asking "Why?" or "How?" or "What is the meaning of that?"

So, with disclaimers firmly in place, what follows is an effort to say something about what's behind the words in the book. An attempt to ask and find answers to the question: What did thirty-six conversations with thirty-six Presbyterians—listening to them talk about their lives in general and the church in particular—evoke: What does what they say to the church?

For one thing, listening to them kindled a large helping of pride. Pride in people whose faith runs so deep; pride in being part of such a family. In one set of words or another, all of them made it plain that faith in God, lived out in the Presbyterian church, is for them foundational.

The listening stirred a sense of people's generosity. They gave of their time most freely. Generosity with time is something different from generosity with money. I heard a lawyer long ago (before we became aware of the unfairness of some pronouns) pay tribute to his pastor in words something like this: "Time is the richest gift a man has to give. He only has a certain amount of it, and he cannot increase it. He cannot use it twice, and once given, it can never be gotten back." The quote comes to mind in reflecting with continuing wonder that people will give their time and tell their stories to a mere acquaintance or, in some cases, a total stranger. There's something remarkably trusting and generous in that.

These people are thinkers—a trait that I believe they have in common with most Presbyterians. To discern such a fact is not great insight, but to note it is important.

One of the questions I often asked in interview/conversations, intended as a kind of common thread, was, "What keeps you in the Presbyterian church?" In varying words, the answer almost always was basically akin to that of a young woman in Colorado who quickly replied, "The real reason I'm Presbyterian is that I'm not pressured on what to believe."

Don't misunderstand. Belief is important to these Presbyterians, and strongly held. It runs very deep in them. Strongly held faith, these conversations repersuaded me, is a signature, a label, a tenet of being, in the family of Presbyterians.

They live mostly in their congregations, these three dozen, as surely do most of their kin who make up the PC(USA). When they speak of the church, it is, in most cases, a reference to the congregation of people with whom they worship on Sundays. Their identity is so dominantly local that any national, synod, or presbytery official or staff member courts trouble who forgets it.

Yet they do not support the naysayer notion that there is great and widespread anger at the larger church. General Assembly, synod, and presbytery levels are not so much disliked as little-known.

Members know they are part of a larger family, but only vaguely so in many cases. Even ruling elders frequently profess little familiarity with regional or national activities. But those members who have had some involvement in the larger church tend to say good words about it.

Insofar as line of familiarity and loyalty exist, they run, in descending order, from congregation to General Assembly to presbytery to synod.

They are grateful to, and for, the church, however they perceive it. One of them, a Vermonter, used words I've a hunch the others would endorse: "I don't think for a moment the Presbyterian church is perfect, but no human nor human institution is . . . the Presbyterian church has given me uncountable riches."

Possibly the strongest thought about the church that these conversations turned up is that of confidence, of hope. In as many different sets of words, there were expressions of conviction that the church will survive the ordeals of the present, as it has those of the past. Some think it needs renewal, some reenergizing, some attention to its roots, some more commitment to causes. Some believe it needs to reshape its worship practices, some its methods of reaching out to potential new members or to young people. Some predict that the church of the near or distant future will be vastly different. But all believe it will survive.

One more thing: Old or young, whatever the background and whatever geography, they all have interesting stories to tell. Which conjures up the notion that the stories of so-called ordinary Presbyterians may be kind of glue for holding the family together. It may be that telling and listening to each other's stories could be a curative for much that besets us.

Because they are stories of faith. I keep coming back to that word; it keeps coming back to me.

That's some of what I learned. Or maybe relearned, in the miles and hours and satisfaction of talking with—and mostly listening to—a remarkable set of dear hearts who also are known as Presbyterians.